D1357511

World Timbers

VOLUME TWO

WORLD TIMBERS

VOLUME TWO

NORTH & SOUTH AMERICA

[including Central America and the West Indies]

Compiled and edited by

B. J. RENDLE

LONDON: ERNEST BENN LIMITED

UNIVERSITY OF TORONTO PRESS

First published in this form 1969
by Ernest Benn Limited
Bouverie House, Fleet Street, London, EC4
Published in Canada and United States by
University of Toronto Press,
8020 1667 7

© Ernest Benn Limited 1969
Printed in Great Britain
510–48002–0

Contents

[*continued on page 6*]

Contents [*continued from page 5*]

South American Timbers
[including Central America and the West Indies]

Introduction

A feature of the journal *Wood*, since it commenced publication in 1936, has been the two series of colour plates of timbers accompanied by technical information on their properties and uses.

The first series, under the name WOOD SPECIMENS, covered the years 1936–1960; this was followed by the current series of WORLD TIMBERS. A selection of one hundred of the WOOD SPECIMENS was reproduced in book form in 1949[1] and a second volume appeared in 1957[2]. A disadvantage of these volumes, which are now out of print, was the haphazard arrangement of the timbers. The present proprietors of *Wood* have decided to re-issue selected plates from both series (WOOD SPECIMENS and WORLD TIMBERS) in a more systematic arrangement with the technical information revised to bring it up to date and in line with the series now appearing in *Wood*.

The first volume of WORLD TIMBERS, covering the continents of Europe and Africa, was published in March, 1969. Volume 2 covers North and South America, Central America and the West Indies, and Volume 3 will deal with Asia, Australia and New Zealand.

The timbers have been selected primarily for their economic importance or interest on the world market. Many of the species included in the earlier publication are no longer in general use. On the other hand the opening up of new areas of supply, combined with improvements in methods of production and processing and changes in utilisation, have resulted in other species assuming commercial importance.

The Colour Plates

Most of the plates in this volume originally appeared in *Wood* between 1936 and 1969. Fourteen are new and are now published for the first time. Thanks are due to those timber importers and others who kindly supplied the specimens used to prepare the plates.

Care has been taken to ensure that the specimens are representative of the timbers concerned. However, anyone with a knowledge of wood is well aware of the limitations of a single specimen or a single illustration. Allowance must be made for the normal variations in colour, grain and texture, which are so characteristic of wood, as also the differences in appearance due to the method of converting a log (by sawing through-and-through, or by quartering, rotary peeling, slicing, etc.) and the different types of decorative figure that are found in abnormal logs.

Some indication of the variation that is to be expected and the changes in colour that occur with the passage of time is given in the description accompanying each plate. It is advisable, however, when choosing wood for high-class decorative work —whether solid timber or veneer—to examine and select material from the merchant's actual stocks. Small samples may be misleading.

The Technical Descriptions

The technical information accompanying the plates is presented in a form designed to appeal to those who are interested in timber but are not specialists in wood technology. The publishers believe that it will be particularly useful to architects and their clients and those members of the timber trade, the timber-using industries and the general public who do not have access to a representative collection of timber specimens and a library of standard reference books on timber.

Each timber is described in such detail as its importance seems to warrant. The aim is to indicate its outstanding characteristics and to bring out the practical significance of the information presented.

---

[1] Wood Specimens—100 Reproductions in Colour. The Nema Press, London, 1949.
[2] A Second Collection of Wood Specimens—100 Reproductions in Colour. The Tothill Press Ltd., London, 1957.

In selecting a timber for a particular purpose some knowledge of the supply position is essential. The section headed *Distribution and supplies* gives the geographical distribution in broad terms, emphasising the principal sources of supply, with some indication of the quantity and sizes available and whether the timber is commonly stocked in the form of logs, lumber, veneer, etc., or in special sizes such as flooring strips, or is likely to be obtainable only to special order. The notes on supplies refer particularly to Britain. Although the supply position is subject to change and varies in different parts of the world, it is believed this information will be useful to intending purchasers. Before making a final selection, however, it may be advisable to consult a timber merchant.

The main part of each description consists of practical information on the technical properties of the timber in simple language with the minimum of technical terms. The information is largely based on the results of investigations carried out by research laboratories and the source of the data is hereby acknowledged. A list of the principal publications consulted—and recommended to those readers who require more detailed information—is on page 143.

The terms used to classify the timbers in respect of certain technical properties are the standard terms adopted by the Forest Products Research Laboratory of Great Britain and defined in the Laboratory's Handbook of Hardwoods (1956) and Handbook of Softwoods (1960).

Seasoning and movement. In a book of this kind it is considered sufficient to state briefly the rate at which a timber dries and the degree of deterioration due to distortion, splitting, etc., to be expected. In some cases the recommended kiln-drying schedule is mentioned; particulars of these schedules are given in Forest Products Research Laboratory Leaflet No. 42. As applied to timber, the term movement means the tendency to shrink or swell in service under varying atmospheric conditions. On the basis of a standard method of measuring the dimensional changes of small timber samples over a predetermined range of atmospheric humidity, timbers are arbitrarily classified as having small, medium or large movement values (for particulars see FPRL Leaflet No. 47).

Strength and bending properties. It is not easy to generalise about the strength of a timber because this term covers a number of specific strength properties, or mechanical properties as they are sometimes called. It has been found more convenient, therefore, to indicate the strength of each timber by comparing it with a well-known standard timber and by mentioning any outstanding mechanical property. Classification according to steam-bending properties is based on the minimum bending radius of sound, clear specimens one-inch thick. Timbers are classified in one of five groups ranging from Very poor to Very good (for particulars see FPRL Leaflet No. 45).

Durability and preservative treatment. The term durability is used to describe the natural resistance of a timber to fungal decay and insect attack. For convenience timbers are roughly classified in five grades intended to indicate the useful life of the timber in contact with the ground, as follows:

Perishable (5 years or less), e.g., birch, balsa and the *sapwood* of most timbers.
Non-durable (5–10 years), e.g., basswood, maple, white pine, spruce.
Moderately durable (10–15 years), e.g., walnut, Douglas fir.
Durable (15–25 years), e.g., white oak, western red cedar.
Very durable (more than 25 years), e.g., teak, greenheart.

Resistance to the attack of specific insects (and also marine borers) is mentioned where appropriate.

It is sometimes more convenient to use a non-durable timber treated with a preservative than a naturally durable timber. Some timbers are readily impregnated with preservatives whereas others are more or less impermeable and cannot be given a satisfactory treatment. Where a long service life is required under conditions favourable to decay or insect attack it is important to choose a timber that will absorb an adequate amount of preservative. The terms used to describe amenability to preservative treatment are self-explanatory. It should be noted that they refer to *heartwood*; the sapwood is usually much more permeable.

Uses. The section on uses cites some of the more typical uses of the timber in question and, where appropriate, indicates its suitability for various purposes in comparison with other species, bearing in mind that suitability may depend as much on economic factors, such as availability, price and sizes, as the technical and aesthetic properties of the timber. This section reflects the editor's personal knowledge of timber utilisation in Britain but much of the information will be found to apply in other countries as well.

Metrication
Great Britain is now committed to the adoption of the metric system in commerce and industry. It will be some time before the change is complete in all fields and during the transitional period both foot/inch measure and metric will be in use for timber. To meet this situation numerical data are expressed in metric units as well as in the traditional form. The figures given are approximate; for greater accuracy the conventional British units of measurement used for timber may be converted to metric units by using the appropriate conversion factor as follows:

To convert inches to mm. multiply by 25·4

,, ,, feet to m. multiply by 0·305

,, ,, lb. to kg. multiply by 0·454

,, ,, lb./ft.³ to kg./m.³ multiply by 16·02.

ERRATA

page 41   **Poplar** *for* Quarter cut *read* Flat cut

page 71   **Redwood** *for* Flat cut *read* Burr

page 75   **Spruce, Sitka** the diagrams at foot should be transposed

North American Timbers

HARDWOODS

Ash

[various species of *Fraxinus*]

The principal commercial species, known as white ash, is *Fraxinus americana*, which is the main source of American tough ash as distinct from soft ash or cabinet ash.

Distribution and supplies. White ash is a well-formed tree, commonly up to 18 m. (60 ft.) in height and 0·9 m. (3 ft.) in diameter, though supplies are derived mainly from smaller second-growth trees. It is widely distributed throughout the eastern United States and south-eastern Canada. Oregon ash grows along the Pacific coast. Limited quantities of American ash are shipped to Europe in the form of square-edged lumber and dimension stock.

General description. White ash is similar in appearance to European ash. On the average it is a little less dense, about 0·66 (41 lb./ft.^{3}) in the seasoned condition. Timber for sports goods, tool handles, motor body building and similar purposes is graded as tough ash, while the softer, lighter material, which is more suitable for furniture and joinery, is sold as soft ash.

Seasoning and movement. Air seasoning is straightforward and fairly rapid, but existing shakes will probably open more. Ash can be kiln-dried easily if temperatures are kept low, otherwise distortion and end splitting may occur. Distortion can be removed by reconditioning with high-temperature steam. Ash is only moderately stable in varying humidity.

Strength and bending properties. Material graded as tough resembles European ash in strength and bends well, though laboratory tests indicate an inferiority for steam bending compared with ash grown in Britain. Soft ash has comparatively poor strength properties and is usually unsuitable for the handles of striking tools or for the stressed parts of wooden structures. Oregon ash is generally inferior to white ash in strength.

Durability and preservative treatment. Ash is not resistant to fungal decay. The sapwood is liable to be attacked by powder-post (*Lyctus*) beetles and by the common furniture beetle. Heartwood does not respond very well to preservative treatment.

Working and finishing properties. Like European ash, tough American ash is fairly easy to work for a hardwood of medium density and takes a good finish with only a moderate dulling effect on cutting edges. Soft ash is naturally easier to work. It gives good results with stain and polish and can be glued satisfactorily under well-controlled conditions.

Uses. Selected American ash is used for the same purposes as European ash, notably for sports goods, the handles of striking tools such as axes and hammers, and garden tools such as spades, rakes and hoes, and for motor body building and agricultural machinery. Some specifications for handle stock call for timber with 2–7 rings/cm. (5–17 rings/in.). Soft ash is used for cooperage, shopfitting, and, because of its light colour and attractive grain, interior joinery and panelling.

12

Ash

Flat cut

Reproduced actual size

Basswood

[Tilia americana and allied species]*

Distribution and supplies. Basswood is the North American counterpart of the European lime or linden (*Tilia vulgaris* and allied species). It is a medium-sized tree of the eastern regions of the USA and Canada, commonly growing to a height of about 20 m. (65 ft.) and a diameter of 0·6–0·75 m. (2–2½ ft.). The timber is exported to Europe in limited quantities for special purposes.

General description. In colour, grain and texture basswood resembles European lime, being creamy-white to light-brown, usually straight grained with a fine, even texture, devoid of any decorative feature; it is appreciably lighter and softer than the European timber, the average density being about 0·43 (27 lb./ft.^{3}) in the seasoned condition. The sapwood is sometimes marketed as white basswood.

Seasoning and movement. Basswood dries without much deterioration and exhibits little movement in service.

Strength and bending properties. A soft, light timber with corresponding strength properties generally similar to those of poplar. It is reputed to have poor bending properties.

Durability and preservative treatment. A non-durable timber susceptible to infestation by furniture beetles. Permeable to preservatives.

Working and finishing properties. Basswood is exceptionally easy to work with either hand or machine tools, but has a very slight dulling effect on cutting edges. The timber finishes smoothly and cleanly if tools are kept reasonably sharp. It takes stain and polish well and can be glued satisfactorily.

Uses. Basswood is favoured for products made of wood in the natural condition, especially when a clean, attractive appearance, light weight and freedom from taste and odour are essential, for example, food containers and wood-wool. The wood is particularly useful in precision working and for stability, e.g., in piano keys and model making. It is excellent for hand carving, as it is soft and cuts with a clean, smooth surface in all directions of the grain.

Basswood

Quarter cut

Reproduced actual size

Beech

[Fagus grandifolia]

Distribution and supplies. The North American counter partof European beech is distributed generally over the eastern United States and south-eastern Canada, being particularly common in the central and middle Atlantic states. Mature forest-grown trees are commonly 30 m. (100 ft.) or more in height and 1 m. (say, 3 ft.) or more in diameter.

General description. A general-utility hardwood of plain appearance, usually straight grained and of fine, even texture, similar to European beech. Nearly white to pale-brown, sometimes with a reddish-brown heartwood. The lighter and darker coloured wood is sometimes marketed as white beech and red beech respectively. Average density about 0·72 (45 lb./ft.^{3}) in the seasoned condition. Odourless and tasteless.

Seasoning and movement. Beech shrinks considerably and requires careful drying to minimise distortion and splitting. It has a comparatively large movement in service.

Strength and bending properties. Beech has strength properties similar to oak; it has a comparatively high resistance to shock and is exceptionally good for steam bending.

Durability and preservative treatment. The wood is not very resistant to decay but readily absorbs preservatives.

Working and finishing properties. Though hard, beech works fairly readily and takes a smooth finish, particularly in turning. Close control of gluing conditions is required.

Uses. Because of the wider choice of indigenous timbers, beech is less important in America than is European beech in Western and Central Europe. It is considered inferior to maple and birch but is used for similar purposes where a timber with good all-round strength properties and good working qualities is required, notably for flooring, chairs and furniture frames, turnery, cooperage, boxes and crates and, after preservative treatment, for railway ties (sleepers).

16

Beech

Flat cut

 Reproduced actual size

Birch, Yellow

[principally *Betula alleghaniensis,* formerly *B. lutea*]

Distribution and supplies. Yellow birch is the most important American species of birch. It is common in the eastern regions of Canada and the USA, reaching a height of about 20 m. (say, 60–70 ft.) with a cylindrical bole of 0·6 m. (2 ft.) diameter. Timber for the export market is shipped mainly from Canada (Canadian or Quebec birch), as square-edged lumber in widths of 150 mm. and up, average 225 mm. (6 in. and up, average 9 in.), in lengths of 2.4 m. (8 ft.) and up and as flooring strips and dimension stock and in log form for the manufacture of plywood. Decorative veneers are available. Sweet birch (*Betula lenta*) is also included in commercial shipments of yellow birch.

General description. Yellow birch is harder, denser and slightly darker in colour than European birch. It is generally straight grained and of plain appearance but some logs have a curly or wavy grain, yielding a decorative figure. The heartwood varies from light to dark reddish-brown. The almost white sapwood is sometimes marketed separately as white birch (not to be confused with paper birch (*B. papyrifera*), see below). The density of yellow birch in the seasoned condition averages about 0·69 (43 lb./ft.^{3}). The wood is odourless and tasteless.

Seasoning and movement. The timber dries fairly slowly with little degrade. Air seasoning as a preliminary to kiln-drying is recommended. Shrinkage in seasoning is considerable and the movement of the seasoned timber in service is classed as large.

Strength and bending properties. Strength properties are above average; in toughness and resistance to shock yellow birch is almost equal to ash. Compared with European birch it is stronger and stiffer in bending and also harder and more resistant to compression parallel to the grain. It is very good for steam bending.

Durability and preservative treatment. The timber is classed as perishable, being susceptible to fungal decay and insect attack. It is only moderately resistant to impregnation, however, and so can be treated satisfactorily with wood preservatives.

Working and finishing properties. Straight-grained material works satisfactorily with hand and machine tools and does not dull the cutting edges of tools unduly. It takes a smooth, silky finish from the tool and is particularly good for turning. Some tearing may occur when the grain is irregular unless the cutting angle is reduced to 15° or less. The timber stains well and gives good results with the usual finishing treatments. Close control of gluing conditions is required.

Uses. Yellow birch is used principally for furniture, interior finish, boxes and crates and plywood. As flooring, straight-grained material wears evenly without surface breakdown and is suitable for use in public buildings such as schools and hospitals. Before the second world war Canadian yellow birch was widely used in Britain in the furniture industry (for chair parts and upholstery frames), for agricultural implements, turnery, high-grade plywood for aircraft and other exacting purposes, and laminated bent work.

Other species of interest. *The paper birch or white birch (*B. papyrifera*) of eastern Canada and the USA more closely resembles European birch than yellow birch, being white in colour and comparatively light in weight. It is a good turnery wood, useful for spools, bobbins, dowels and woodware where a clean, white appearance is required.*

18

Birch

Quarter cut

Reproduced actual size

Flat cut

19

Cherry

[Prunus serotina]

Distribution and supplies. The wild black cherry of the eastern regions of the USA and Canada is the North American counterpart of European cherry. In the Appalachian hardwood region, where it attains its best development, it grows to a height of 30 m. (100 ft.) with a well-shaped trunk 1–1·5 m. (say, 3–5 ft.) in diameter. Though nowhere plentiful, the timber is regularly utilised in the USA and Canada and has been sporadically imported into Britain in small quantities, as square-edged lumber for furniture manufacture.

General description. The sapwood is yellowish and much paler than the brownish or greenish-brown heartwood, which deepens on exposure to a rich reddish-brown mahogany shade with a golden lustre. The wood has a faint aromatic scent which is not permanent. It is of medium density, averaging in the air-dry state about 0·58 (36 lb./ft.³), i.e., about the same as European cherry. The texture is fine and uniform and the grain is usually straight.

Seasoning and movement. With reasonable care the timber seasons satisfactorily both naturally and artificially without excessive shrinkage, though the tangential shrinkage is nearly double the radial, so that warping may be troublesome if attempt is made to hasten the drying unduly. It is reputed to hold its place exceptionally well when manufactured.

Strength and bending properties. Like European cherry, the wood is tough and strong, similar to yellow birch in these respects. It is stiff and resistant to bending and splitting. It has not been subjected to standard steam-bending tests but can be expected to be very good for this purpose, in the same class as beech and ash.

Durability. It is reported to be moderately resistant to decay.

Working and finishing properties. Straight-grained stock works easily in sawing and planing if tools are kept sharp and plane irons are ground to a suitable cutting angle, around 25°. The wood finishes very smoothly and turns satisfactorily, responding well to finishing treatments and taking an excellent polish.

Uses. In America cherry is well known as a high-quality furniture timber in the mahogany class. Latterly it has been largely used for printers' blocks for electrotypes on account of its stability in service. In Britain it has been used to a limited extent for furniture, fancy articles and interior woodwork.

Cherry

Flat cut

Reproduced actual size

Quarter cut

Elm, Rock

[Ulmus thomasi]

Distribution and supplies. A medium-sized tree of limited occurrence in the eastern regions of both Canada and the USA, 15–21 m. (50–70 ft.) in height, 0·3–0·6 m. (1–2 ft.) in diameter. The timber is traditionally shipped to Britain, mainly from Canada, as round logs for conversion to special sizes.

General description. Rock elm is light-brown with no sharp distinction between sapwood and heartwood. It is distinguished from other commercial species of elm by its straight grain, fine texture and greater strength and density, average about 0·78 (49 lb./ft.^{3}) in the seasoned condition.

Seasoning and movement. It is inclined to check and twist in seasoning. Shrinkage in drying is said to be high and it is probably not particularly stable in service.

Strength and bending properties. Rock elm is outstanding for its toughness and resistance to shock, being superior to ash and almost as good as hickory in these respects. Compared with wych elm it is harder and stronger in bending and compression along the grain and about equal in stiffness and resistance to splitting. It is well known for its steam-bending properties and is classed as very good.

Durability and preservative treatment. Like other species of elm, rock elm is not durable under conditions favouring fungal attack and is not readily impregnated with preservatives.

Working and finishing properties. The wood is fairly hard to work by hand but gives satisfactory results in most machining operations, taking a clean, smooth finish from the tool. It has good nailing and screwing properties and takes stain, varnish, paints and polish well.

Uses. Because of its outstanding resistance to wear and tear, rock elm has long been favoured for dock and wharf construction and for ships' fenders. It is a traditional timber for the bent frames of small boats and for stringers, rubbing strips and belting, but its use in boat building has declined because of the susceptibility to decay. Other uses include agricultural machinery, ladder rungs and gymnasium equipment.

Elm, Rock

Flat cut

   Reproduced actual size

Elm, White

[Ulmus americana]

Distribution and supplies. The American or white elm is the most important species of North American elm for timber production, its natural range covering the eastern half of the USA and Canada. It is commonly 18–25 m. (60–80 ft.) high with a diameter of 1–1·25 m. (3–4 ft.).

General description. The timber has a general resemblance to English elm but tends to be straighter in the grain. The wide sapwood is pale in colour, the heartwood brown, sometimes with a reddish tinge. It is typically coarser in texture, softer and lighter in weight than rock elm, the average density being about 0·61 (38 lb./ft.^{3}), seasoned, though selected dense material approaches rock elm in this respect.

Seasoning and movement. It is reported to season readily with medium shrinkage but, like other species of elm, is probably not particularly stable in service.

Strength and bending properties. The general run of the timber is inferior to rock elm in strength properties, though selected dense grades of white elm approximate to average rock elm. It is considerably stronger than English elm, and is classed as very good for steam bending.

Durability and preservative treatment. White elm is classed as non-durable and is inferior to rock elm in this respect. The heartwood is believed to be moderately resistant to preservative treatment.

Working and finishing properties. The timber works fairly easily with hand and machine tools; sawn surfaces are inclined to be woolly but can be finished smoothly. It takes nails and screws well and gives good results with the usual finishing treatments.

Uses. Large quantities of white elm are used in the USA and Canada in the slack cooperage industry, for staves, heading and hoops, and as veneers for cheese boxes and other veneer products. It is also used for furniture, caskets (coffins), agricultural machinery and as a substitute for rock elm.

Elm, White

Flat cut

 Reproduced actual size

Gum, Red

[Liquidambar styraciflua]

Timber derived from the tree known as sweet gum is usually marketed in the USA as red gum (the heartwood) and sap gum (the sapwood). Before the second world war the heartwood was known in Britain as satin walnut and the sapwood as hazel pine.

Distribution and supplies. Sweet gum is an important timber tree in the south-eastern United States, where it grows to a height of 24–30 m. (80–100 ft.) with a long smooth bole 0·6–1·5 m. (2–5 ft.) in diameter. The timber is in good supply. Formerly it was exported to Britain and can still be supplied to special order.

General description. The wide sapwood is nearly white, the heartwood reddish-brown with a satin lustre, sometimes beautifully marked with irregular dark streaks. The texture is fine and uniform, the grain irregularly interlocked. The average density is about 0·56 (35 lb./ft.^{3}) in the seasoned condition.

Technical properties. Because of the irregular grain the timber must be dried with care to minimise distortion. It is rated as moderately hard and strong, fairly easy to work, finishing very smoothly, and glues well. It is not highly resistant to decay.

Uses. In the USA, as lumber, veneer and plywood, this species is used for a wide range of purposes, notably for furniture and interior woodwork, boxes and crates. Under the name of satin walnut, it was formerly a popular wood for furniture in Britain.

Gum

Flat cut

Reproduced two-thirds actual size

Hickory

[various species of *Carya*]

Commercial hickory comes from species of *Carya* with exceptionally tough wood, namely *C. glabra, C. tomentosa, C. laciniosa* and *C. ovata*. The other species are collectively known as pecan. Unless stated otherwise, the following description refers to commercial hickory.

Distribution and supplies. Hickories occur mainly in south-eastern Canada and the eastern United States. They are medium-sized to large trees with straight cylindrical boles clear of branches to a height of 10 to 18 m. (say, 30–60 ft.) with diameters up to 1 m. (say, 3 ft.) but the best timber is obtained from smaller, second-growth trees. The timber is extensively utilised in the USA and Canada and is shipped overseas, mainly as dimension stock or in a semi-manufactured condition.

General description. Hickory resembles ash but has a reddish-brown heartwood. Where appearance is a consideration the white sapwood (known as white hickory) is sometimes preferred to the heartwood (red hickory). Like ash, hickory is ring porous, i.e., the pores of the spring wood form a well-defined zone or ring. The densest, toughest timber is obtained from quickly grown, wide-ringed trees; it has an average density of about 0·82 (51 lb./ft.^{3}) when dry, i.e., considerably denser than ash. The grain is usually straight but sometimes wavy or irregular.

Seasoning. Hickory can be kiln-dried satisfactorily although with some tendency to end-check; FPRL kiln schedule E has been suggested.

Strength and bending properties. Hickory is outstanding among temperate hardwoods for its combination of high bending strength, stiffness, hardness and shock resistance. It is particularly resistant to suddenly applied loads and almost 100 per cent superior to ash in this respect; in other properties it is generally 25–35 per cent stronger. Although pale wood is often preferred, sapwood and coloured heartwood of similar density are equally strong. Hickory has excellent steam-bending properties.

Durability and preservative treatment. Hickory has little resistance to fungi; the white sapwood is especially vulnerable. It is sometimes damaged by pinhole and longhorn borers and, once dry, the sapwood is susceptible to powder-post beetle attack. The wood is moderately resistant to preservative treatment.

Working and finishing properties. Dense, wide-ringed wood is fairly hard to work, with appreciable blunting effect on tools. It usually machines cleanly but a 20° cutting angle is advisable where irregular grain is present. Close control of gluing conditions is required.

Uses. Selected, straight-grained hickory is the first choice for handles of striking tools, particularly hammer and pick handles and axe helves, and for picking sticks in the textile industry, railway shunting poles and highly stressed parts of agricultural machinery. It has been replaced by steel for golf clubs but is still used in a wide range of heavier sports goods where a stronger wood than ash is required. In the USA and Canada it is used for vehicle body building and for bent work, where ash would be employed in Europe. Selected heavy pecan is used in the USA for handles and flooring. Lower-grade hickory and pecan are used in pallets.

28

Hickory

Quarter cut

Reproduced actual size

Magnolia

[Magnolia grandiflora, M. virginiana and *M. acuminata]*

Distribution and supplies. The North American species of magnolia furnishing commercial timber are found in the hardwood region of the south-eastern United States. *Magnolia grandiflora* is reported to reach a height of 40 m. (130 ft.) and a diameter of 1·5 m. (nearly 5 ft.). The timber is of local importance in the USA.

General description. Magnolia is a greenish-grey or brownish timber resembling American whitewood (yellow poplar) (*Liriodendron tulipifera*). In commercial practice the wood is sometimes mixed with whitewood, though it tends to be denser, on average about 0·56 (35 lb./ft.³). It has a fine, uniform texture and is generally straight grained with no decorative features.

Technical properties. The strength and other properties of magnolia are about average for its density. It has good working, finishing and gluing properties, but is not resistant to decay.

Uses. As a light- to medium-weight wood of plain appearance and with good working qualities, magnolia is used principally in furniture manufacture and interior woodwork and as a substitute for whitewood.

30

Magnolia

Flat cut

 Reproduced actual size

Maple

[various species of *Acer*]

The American species of maple fall into two groups so far as their timber is concerned. The hard maple or rock maple group comprises the sugar maple (*Acer saccharum*) and the black maple (*A. nigrum*). The remaining species are classed as soft maple; they include the red maple (*A. rubrum*), the silver maple (*A. saccharinum*) and the Pacific maple (*A. macrophyllum*).

HARD MAPLE

Distribution and supplies. Hard maple is of common occurrence in the eastern hardwood region of the USA and Canada. After yellow birch it is the most important hardwood in Canada, judged on the basis of utility and availability. Trees are commonly 24–28 m. (say, 80–90 ft.) high and 0·5–0·75 m. (20–30 in.) in diameter. The timber is in good supply and is exported as square-edged lumber up to 400 mm. (16 in.) wide, flooring strips and flooring blocks, roughly turned blocks for the manufacture of shoe lasts, as decorative veneer and in log form.

General description. In appearance, hard maple resembles the closely allied English sycamore (*A. pseudoplatanus*, not to be confused with American sycamore, *Platanus occidentalis*) but is appreciably harder and heavier, average density 0·72 (45 lb./ft.^{3}) in the seasoned condition. The wide, creamy-white sapwood is not sharply defined from the heartwood which, however, usually has a reddish tinge. Large, old trees sometimes have a dark-brown heart. The wood has a fine, even texture and a natural lustre. The fine lines marking the growth rings give rise to a distinctive figure on flat-sawn surfaces. The grain is usually straight but sometimes wavy or curly grain is present, producing a highly decorative figure. Bird's eye figure is most commonly associated with hard maple.

Seasoning and movement. Hard maple dries slowly but without difficulty, though there is considerable shrinkage. Movement in service is classed as medium.

Strength and bending properties. Strength properties are of a high order. The wood is harder and stiffer than beech, more resistant to splitting and withstands shock loads better. It is outstanding for its resistance to abrasion, wearing smoothly with the minimum of surface breakdown, and is rated very good for steam bending.

Durability and preservative treatment. A non-durable timber, resistant to impregnation though the wide sapwood is permeable. Seasoned timber is susceptible to attack by furniture beetles unless treated with an insecticide.

Working and finishing properties. This is not a particularly easy timber to work and takes the keen edges off cutting tools fairly quickly; in fact, it is slightly harder to work than sycamore. In sawing dry timber there is a tendency to tooth vibration and in planing the wood tends to ride on the cutters. When irregular grain is present the surface is liable to pick up but this can be avoided if the cutting angle is reduced to 20°. Hard maple is excellent for lathe work, but tends to burn in end-grain cutting, e.g., in drilling and cross-cutting. It glues satisfactorily and responds well to staining, painting and other finishing treatments.

Uses. Hard maple is valued particularly for its strength and resistance to wear, combined with a good appearance. It is one of the best timbers for flooring, both for heavy industrial traffic, as in warehouses and factories, and for ballrooms, bowling alleys, squash courts, etc. It is unsurpassed for shoe lasts. Other exacting outlets

[*continued on page 34*]

32

Maple

Flat cut (plain)

Reproduced actual size

Flat cut (blister figure)

Reproduced actual size

33

MAPLE [*continued from page 32*]

include turned goods such as bobbins and spools, machinery parts, motor body building, sports goods and musical instruments, notably piano actions. Veneers of figured wood are in demand for decorative work; plain veneers make a high-grade plywood.

SOFT MAPLE

Soft maple has a similar range of distribution to hard maple but extends further south and is also found along the Pacific coast. The wood resembles hard maple in appearance but is not so lustrous and is considerably softer and lighter (the average density varies between 0·53 and 0·61 (33 and 38 lb./ft.^{3}) according to species) and correspondingly inferior in strength and easier to work. Soft maple is utilised locally in much the same way as hard maple but where hardness and strength are not of prime importance.

Maple

Rotary cut (Bird's eye figure)

 Reproduced two-thirds actual size

Oak, Red

[various species of *Quercus*]

The American oaks comprise two major commercial groups, the white oaks and the red oaks. A third group, the evergreen or so-called live oaks, is of minor importance as timber.

Distribution and supplies. Commercial red oak comprises ten or more species, not usually differentiated on the market. One species, the northern red oak, is an important source of timber in Canada. In the USA the range of the group covers the eastern half of the country; red oak lumber is in good supply in the same dimensions as white oak.

General description. Heartwood of red oak is typically pinkish- or reddish-brown. It has a coarser texture than white oak, due to the open pores, and the figure of quarter-cut material is considered to be less attractive than that of white oak. Red oak from the northern states is of comparatively slow growth, resembling northern white oak in this respect; timber from the southern states is generally of more rapid growth and consequently harder, heavier and coarser in texture. In the red oak group as a whole, density varies in much the same way as white oak, averages for the principal species varying from 0·66 to 0·77 (41–48 lb./ft.^{3}) in the seasoned condition.

Seasoning and movement. Compared with European oak and American white oak of similar grade, red oak tends to be more refractory in seasoning, with a strong tendency to warp and check, particularly southern red oak. Movement in service is about the same as white oak, i.e., medium.

Strength and bending properties. Red oak varies over a similar range to white oak in strength. Like white oak it is commonly used for steam bending.

Durability and preservative treatment. In its resistance to decay, red oak is inferior to European oak and American white oak and is classed as non-durable. Being more permeable, however, it is amenable to preservative treatment.

Working and finishing properties. Red oak is generally considered inferior to white oak.

Uses. Red oak is used for many of the same purposes as white oak with the notable exceptions of tight cooperage and constructional work requiring a high degree of natural durability. For furniture and interior woodwork it is valued less highly than European and American white oak on account of its reddish colour, coarser texture and less attractive figure.

Oak, Red

Flat cut

 Reproduced actual size

37

Oak, White

[various species of *Quercus*]

Distribution and supplies. White oak comes from nine or more species, mainly in the central hardwood region of the USA and adjacent parts of Canada. It is a major commercial timber of North America. The trees vary in size according to species and locality; well-grown specimens have a straight clear bole of 12–15 m. (40–50 ft.), 1 m. or more (say, 3–4 ft.) in diameter. The timber is largely used in the USA and Canada and is exported from the States mainly as kiln-dried, graded, square-edged lumber (plain and figured), flooring strips, flooring blocks and barrel staves. In Britain it is available in widths of 150–350 mm., average 200–250 mm. (6–14, average 8–10 in.), in thicknesses of 25–100 mm. (1–4 in.) and lengths up to 4·8 m. (16 ft.).

General description. American white oak resembles European oak. Being a mixture of species, however, it is more variable in colour, pale yellowish-brown to mid-brown, sometimes with a pinkish tint. It varies also in quality according to locality. Thus oak from Canada and the northern USA is generally less hard and heavy than that from the southern states. Average density is about 0·75 (47 lb./ft.³), seasoned. The grain is usually straight except around knots. The characteristic silver grain figure due to the broad rays is shown to advantage on quarter-cut material. In common with other species of oak, white oak corrodes metals, particularly iron, steel and lead; blue-black discolorations, from the tannic acid in the wood, are liable to develop when it is in contact with iron or iron compounds under damp conditions. Use of non-ferrous metals for fastenings and fittings is recommended; alternatively iron or steel metal work should be galvanised or well painted.

Seasoning and movement. The timber seasons fairly slowly and tends to check and split. Movement in service is rated as medium.

Strength and bending properties. White oak is almost identical with European oak in strength; it ranks fairly high in all strength properties, and is classed as very good for steam bending.

Durability and preservative treatment. The heartwood is renowned for its durability and is commonly used outdoors without preservative treatment. Such treatment is advisable, however, when sapwood is present. The heartwood is extremely resistant to impregnation but the sapwood can be treated under pressure.

Working and finishing properties. Considering its density the timber can be worked fairly readily, taking a smooth finish. It can be glued satisfactorily.

Uses. Because of its good all-round strength and resistance to decay, white oak is used for a wide range of constructional work, including ship and boat building. It is traditional for high-grade furniture, interior woodwork and flooring. Because of its impermeability the timber is suitable for vats and casks for holding liquids such as wine and spirits. Material exported to Europe is selected for the manufacture of furniture, joinery and flooring or in the form of staves for vats and casks, particularly for whisky.

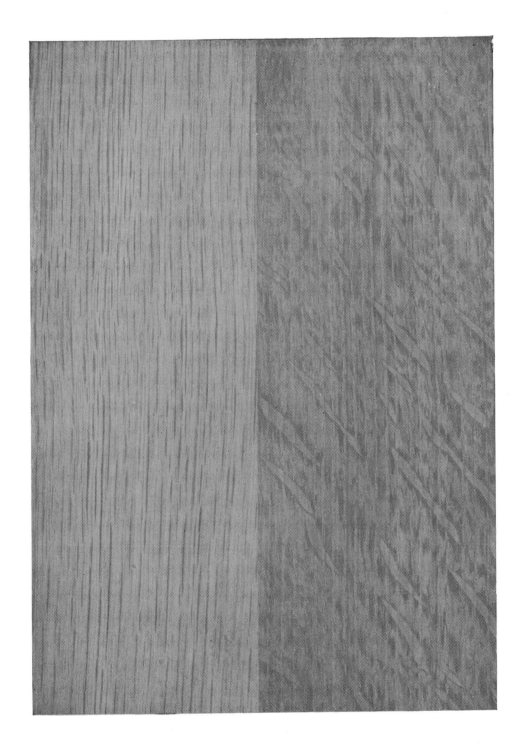

Oak, White

Flat cut

Quarter cut

Reproduced actual size

39

Poplar

[various species of *Populus*]

The North American species of poplar fall into two main groups, the aspens and the cottonwoods. In the American timber trade, however, the lumber is commonly sold as cottonwood and the pulpwood as poplar, irrespective of species. Note that the name poplar is also used for the timber of American whitewood, more commonly known as yellow poplar (*Liriodendron tulipifera*).

Distribution and supplies. The Canadian aspen, which also occurs in the USA, is commonly 15–18 m. (50–60 ft.) in height and 0·2–0·3 m. (8–12 in.) in diameter, occasionally more. The cottonwoods are generally taller, reaching 30 m. (100 ft.) or more in height and 1 m. or more (say, 3–4 ft.) in diameter. Timber of both groups is in good supply as lumber, pulpwood and logs throughout most of Canada and the USA, and fast-growing hybrid poplars are extensively cultivated in North and South America. Canadian aspen is exported to Britain in log form to supplement European supplies of poplar for the manufacture of matches.

General description. Poplar wood is fairly soft and light; the average density for the different species varies between 0·40 and 0·46 (25–29 lb./ft.^{3}), seasoned. It is usually of plain appearance apart from a growth-ring figure on flat-sawn or rotary-cut material, greyish-white to light greyish-brown, sometimes with a reddish tinge, with no sharp distinction between sapwood and heartwood. The grain is usually straight, the texture fine and even (aspen tends to be of finer texture and more lustrous than cottonwood). The wood is odourless and tasteless when well seasoned.

Seasoning. Poplar requires care in seasoning as it is inclined to warp and twist. FPRL kiln schedule E is suggested.

Strength and bending properties. Being soft and light, poplar has a low strength rating, similar to basswood and spruce, but ranks comparatively high in toughness and resistance to shock and wears evenly under abrasion. It is unsuitable for steam bending.

Durability and preservative treatment. All species of poplar are non-durable under damp conditions. Moreover, the heartwood is resistant to impregnation and consequently not amenable to preservative treatment.

Working and finishing properties. The timber works fairly easily and well by both machine and hand, provided sharp, thin-edged tools are used; with dulled cutters there is a tendency for a woolly surface on planing and for the timber to crumble in end-grain cutting. It nails and screws well and presents no difficulty in finishing. The logs peel easily and the wood can be glued and painted without difficulty.

Uses. A major outlet for poplar wood is boxes and crates and wood-wool (excelsior). Logs of suitable size and form are converted to veneer for matches (particularly aspen,) chip baskets for fruit and vegetables, and plywood. The poplars are an important source of wood-pulp.

Poplar

Quarter cut

  Reproduced actual size

Walnut, Black

[Juglans nigra]

Distribution and supplies. Black walnut is characteristic of the eastern United States, being at its best in the central hardwood region; it is also found, to a limited extent, in Canada. It is one of the largest hardwood trees of North America, with a clear bole up to 18 m. (60 ft.) long and 1·8 m. (6 ft.) in diameter, though forest-grown trees of these dimensions are rare, and supplies obtained mostly from smaller trees grown on farms. The timber is available in Britain as square-edged boards 25–100 mm. (1–4 in.) thick, 150–225 mm. (6–9 in.) wide and 1·8–3 m. (6–10 ft.) long, and as veneer.

General description. The timber resembles European walnut in texture but is less variable in colour, and usually darker. The colour is apt to darken with age, whereas European walnut may become paler after prolonged exposure. The sapwood is distinctly paler than the heartwood and varies in width with the age and size of the tree and conditions of growth. The heartwood is typically a uniform dark purplish-brown. It is the darkest hardwood readily available in a wide range of specifications. Burrs sometimes occur and the wood of these and of stumps is often highly figured and is converted to veneers; otherwise the wood is normally straight grained. Density is variable, usually from 0·56 to 0·67 (35–42 lb./ft.³), seasoned.

Seasoning and movement. Black walnut loses moisture slowly when air seasoned but does not usually develop serious distortion or other defect. In a drying kiln it also remains free from distortion but is slow in drying. No pronounced differential shrinkage occurs and the timber is stable in service.

Strength and bending properties. Black walnut is hard, strong, stiff, resists shock and does not splinter. It is suitable for steam bending.

Durability. The wood is moderately resistant to fungal and insect attack, sometimes being attacked by longhorn beetles which may bore in furniture for a long time before discovery.

Working and finishing properties. It is a kindly wood to work with hand and machine tools. Owing to the oily nature it cuts cleanly, especially with small hand tools which leave a fine surface finish. Black walnut is excellent for carving and works well in the lathe, to a smooth finish. Gluing is satisfactory under well-controlled conditions.

Uses. Black walnut is one of the best American woods for furniture, cabinet work and interior decoration and is unsurpassed for gun stocks and rifle butts. In Britain it is often used in place of European walnut which has become scarce.

Other species of interest. *Butternut or white walnut (J. cinerea) resembles black walnut in grain and texture but is lighter in colour, softer and weaker. It is sometimes stained to resemble black walnut.*

42

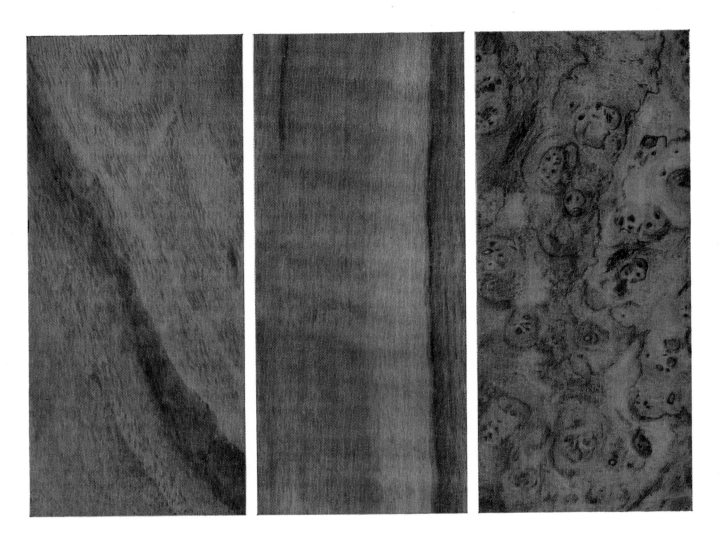

Walnut

Flat cut

Reproduced actual size

Quarter cut

Burr

43

Whitewood or Yellow Poplar

[Liriodendron tulipifera]

The timber is also known as canary wood or canary whitewood (Britain) and as poplar or tulip poplar (USA).

Distribution and supplies. A large, well-proportioned tree of the central hardwood region of the USA, being particularly common in the southern states. The timber is produced in large quantities, mostly for use in the USA and Canada. Before the second world war it was widely used in Britain but has practically disappeared from the market.

General description. A light, soft wood of fine texture, generally straight grained. The heartwood of old forest trees is yellowish-brown, sometimes streaked with purple, green or red, with a narrow, creamy-white sapwood. Second-growth timber has a much larger proportion of white sapwood—hence the name whitewood. The density is variable, from 0·40 (25 lb./ft.³) in old growth to 0·51 (32 lb./ft.³) in second-growth timber.

Technical properties. Whitewood is easy to season and holds its place well in service. It is only moderately strong and is not resistant to decay but has excellent working and finishing properties.

Uses. The timber is used in large quantities in the USA and Canada, for furniture framework and interiors, as core stock for plywood, pianos and television cabinets, and for many other purposes where good working and finishing properties are more important than strength and durability.

Whitewood

Flat cut

Reproduced actual size

North American Timbers

SOFTWOODS

Cedar, Incense

[Libocedrus decurrens]

The name cedar, with qualifications, is commonly applied to any kind of timber with a natural fragrance recalling that of the true cedar of Lebanon (*Cedrus libani*). The cedars of North America have certain other characteristics in common, being fairly soft, easily worked and resistant to decay and insect attack.

Distribution and supplies. The incense cedar is a medium-sized to large tree, usually 25–30 m. (say, 80–100 ft.) in height and about 1 m. (say, 3–4 ft.) in diameter, practically confined to California and Oregon. The timber is available in the form of lumber and as pencil slats.

General description. Incense cedar has a general resemblance to western red cedar, being light-brown with a reddish tinge, a spicy, cedar-like odour and a fine, even texture. It is soft and light, average density about 0·40 (25 lb./ft.³), seasoned. Many trees are affected by a form of rot and the quality of much of the lumber is reduced by pockets of decayed wood. Timber so affected is known as pecky cedar.

Technical properties. The lumber is easy to season with little checking or warping. Strength properties are low, similar to those of western red cedar. The wood is fissile, very easy to work and highly durable.

Uses. Lumber is mainly utilised locally for building purposes, fencing and items of furniture such as clothes chests. It makes good roofing shingles. Most of the high-grade material is converted into slats for the manufacture of pencils as an alternative to pencil cedar (*Juniperus virginiana*) which is in short supply.

Cedar, Incense

Quarter cut

Reproduced actual size

49

Cedar, Pencil or Red

[*Juniperus virginiana* and *J. lucayana*]

Distribution and supplies. The eastern red cedar, as it is known in America (*Juniperus virginiana*) is found in the eastern states and southern Ontario. It is a comparatively small tree, usually 12–15 m. (40–50 ft.) high and 0·3–0·5 m. (say, 1–1½ ft.) in diameter. In the form of pencil slats it was shipped to Britain from Virginia and became known as Virginian pencil cedar to distinguish it from the African pencil cedar (*J. procera*). In recent years supplies have diminished. Another species, the southern red cedar (*J. lucayana*), is of commercial importance in Florida and southern Georgia.

General description. Pencil cedar is a fine-textured, light reddish-brown wood with a characteristic cedar scent, fissile but easy to cut in all directions of the grain. The average density is about 0·53 (33 lb./ft.³) in the seasoned condition. Much of the lumber now available is from small trees and consequently tends to be knotty. Clear, straight-grained stock is normally limited to pieces of small dimension such as pencil slats.

Technical properties. The outstanding technical characteristics of pencil cedar are its high resistance to decay and its excellent working qualities when reasonably free from knots and irregular grain, apart from a liability to split when nailed. Strength properties are generally low. It has very low shrinkage and stays in place well after seasoning.

Uses. The timber of both species is largely used locally for fencing, also for furniture, especially clothes chests and wardrobes on account of its reputation for inhibiting the activity of moths. It is more widely known as possibly the best wood for lead pencils, but owing to shortage of supplies it has been largely replaced by incense cedar and African pencil cedar. The aromatic cedar-wood oil used in toilet preparations is obtained by distillation of sawdust and wood waste.

50

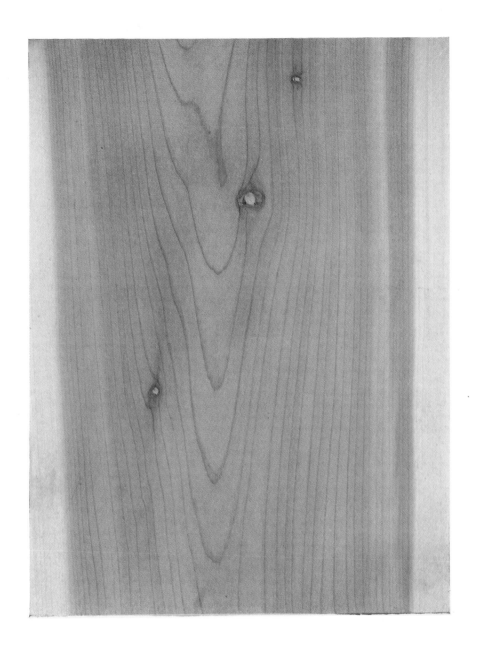

Cedar, Pencil

Flat cut

Reproduced actual size

Cedar, Port Orford

[Chamaecyparis lawsoniana]

Distribution and supplies. Port Orford cedar is an important timber tree in the USA though it has a limited distribution along the coast of Oregon and California. It is a large tree, commonly 40–53 m. (130–175 ft.) high and up to 2 m. (say, 7 ft.) in diameter. In Britain, where it is known as Lawson's cypress, it has been grown on a small scale in plantations but is more familiar as an ornamental tree and as a garden hedge plant. The American timber is not exported in quantity but is obtainable to special order.

General description. The wood is light-yellow to pale-brown with no clear distinction between sapwood and heartwood. It has a fine, even texture, straight grain and a characteristic fragrant, spicy odour. Density in the seasoned condition is about 0·47 (29 lb./ft.^{3}).

Technical properties. Port Orford cedar has exceptionally good technical properties, being highly resistant to decay and easy to work to a smooth finish, though it sometimes shows slight resin exudations. It seasons readily with little tendency to warp and is dimensionally stable in service. It gives good results with paint, stain and other finishing treatments.

Uses. The higher grades are largely used for battery separators and venetian blind slats, also for joinery and furniture interiors (it is reputed to prevent the attack of moth), boat building and matches.

Cedar, Port Orford

Flat cut

 Reproduced actual size

Cedar, Western Red

[*Thuja plicata*]

Distribution and supplies. Western red cedar is an important timber tree of British Columbia and the western United States. It is generally 38–53 m. (125–175 ft.) high and 1–2·5 m. (say, 3–8 ft.) in diameter. The timber is shipped to all parts of North America, and exported in the form of roofing shingles and as lumber in widths of 100 mm. (4 in.) and wider and thicknesses of 25–100 mm. (1–4 in.); lengths are normally 2·4–7·2 m. (8–24 ft.). The species grows well in Britain in plantations and as an ornamental tree.

General description. The heartwood varies from pinkish to dark chocolate-brown, becoming more uniform with age; exposed to the weather it assumes a pleasing silver-grey shade. Western red cedar is exceptionally light in weight; average density is about 0·37 (23 lb./ft.³), seasoned. It is typically straight grained with a uniform but fairly coarse texture and prominent growth rings. Because of its acid nature the wood tends to corrode certain metals, notably iron and steel, and reddish stains may develop where the wood is in contact with iron under damp conditions.

Seasoning and movement. In the form of thin boards, as generally used, the timber seasons readily with little degrade and very little shrinkage. Thicker material is sometimes difficult to dry, and collapse and honeycombing may develop. The movement of seasoned timber is classed as small.

Strength properties. Western red cedar is fairly strong when used as a round pole. In the form of lumber its strength is much lower than most softwoods in common use.

Durability and preservative treatment. This is a much more durable timber than most softwoods in common use. It is resistant to impregnation but despite its high natural durability, preservative treatment is recommended for roofing shingles in Britain.

Working and finishing properties. Western red cedar has exceptionally good working qualities and takes a smooth, satiny finish with sharp tools. Being soft and relatively brittle it is inclined to splinter when worked on end grain and the surface may become ridged when planed with dull cutters. The wood has fairly good nailing properties; hot-dipped galvanised or copper nails should be used. It takes stains and paints well and has good gluing properties.

Uses. The principal use is for roofing shingles and outdoor work requiring durability and light weight. The wood is widely used, unpainted, for greenhouses, portable buildings and weather boarding, and on a smaller scale for interiors. Timber from plantation-grown trees is generally inferior in quality, with numerous small knots. It is useful for poles, fencing, etc.

Other species of interest. *Eastern white cedar or northern white cedar (T. occidentalis) is a tree of eastern Canada and USA. The wood is exceptionally light in weight, density about 0·34 (21 lb./ft.³), similar to western red cedar but lighter in colour (pale-brown) and available only in comparatively small dimensions. It is used locally in the round for poles, fencing, etc., and for light constructional work in situations favouring decay.*

Cedar, Western Red

Quarter cut

 Reproduced two-thirds actual size

Cedar, Yellow or Alaska

[Chamaecyparis nootkatensis]

Distribution and supplies. Yellow cedar is confined to the Pacific coast region of Canada and the USA. It reaches its best development in British Columbia where it is commonly about 24 m. (80 ft.) high and 0·6–0·9 m. (2–3 ft.) in diameter, often larger. The limited supplies are mostly utilised locally, though it has been exported to Britain.

General description. The wood is pale-yellow with a fine, even texture and a usually straight grain. When freshly cut it has an unpleasant odour which does not persist after seasoning. The density in the seasoned condition is about 0·50 (31 lb./ft.³).

Technical properties. Yellow cedar is fairly hard and strong with exceptionally good working and finishing qualities. It shrinks little in drying, is stable in service and is resistant to decay, insect attack and marine borers. A brown discoloration sometimes develops when the wood is in contact with iron or iron compounds under damp conditions.

Uses. Because of its excellent working qualities, stability and freedom from defects, yellow cedar is used for high-class joinery, notably windows and exterior doors, small boats, engineers' patterns, surveyors' poles, cabinet work and carving. It is the principal Canadian wood used for battery separators.

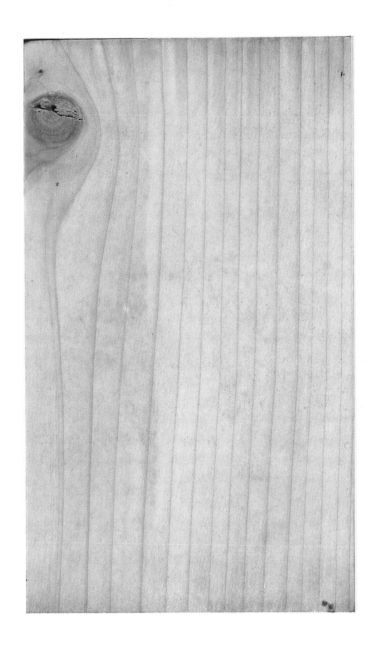

Cedar, Yellow

Quarter cut

   Reproduced actual size

Cypress, Southern

[Taxodium distichum]

Southern cypress is also known as swamp cypress, Louisiana cypress, Gulf cypress, red, yellow and white cypress and simply as cypress. Note that the name cypress strictly refers to species of the botanical genera *Cupressus* and *Chamaecyparis*, e.g., *Cupressus sempervirens*, the Mediterranean cypress, and *Chamaecyparis lawsoniana*, Lawson's cypress, also known as Port Orford cedar.

Distribution and supplies. The tree grows in swamps and on river banks in the Atlantic coastal plain of the USA and is most abundant in the lower Mississippi valley and in Florida. The average size of mature trees is about 30 m. (100 ft.) high and 1–1·5 m. (say, 3–5 ft.) in diameter. It is mainly converted to lumber.

General description. The heartwood varies widely from pale yellowish-brown to dark reddish-brown. Growth rings are strongly marked and tend to be fairly irregular, producing a decorative figure in flat-sawn timber. The wood is greasy to the touch and may have a sour odour but is non-tainting. The average density is about 0·51 (32 lb./ft.^{3}), seasoned.

Technical properties. The timber is reported to season well with moderately small shrinkage, but is difficult to dry in large dimensions. It is similar to Baltic redwood in strength. The heartwood generally is highly resistant to decay, particularly the darker-coloured wood; it is classed as durable. The wood is easily worked and finishes cleanly provided sharp tools are employed. It is stable in service, holds paint and can be glued satisfactorily.

Uses. Southern cypress is used principally for constructional work where resistance to decay is required. It is excellent for weather boarding and roofing shingles. Because of its good working and finishing qualities and attractive appearance, a large proportion of the high-grade lumber is used for interior woodwork such as panelling and doors. Figured wood is sliced to produce decorative veneer, as illustrated. Southern cypress is one of the best timbers for the manufacture of vats and tanks and was formerly used in Britain for this purpose.

Cypress

Flat cut

Reproduced two-thirds actual size

Douglas Fir

[Pseudotsuga menziesii, formerly called *P. taxifolia* and *P. douglasii]*

Sometimes called British Columbia pine, Columbian or Oregon pine.

Distribution and supplies. Douglas fir is the most important timber tree of western Canada and the USA. It has been planted extensively in Britain where it produces timber similar to second-growth material in North America. In its native habitat it commonly grows to a height of 45–60 m. (150–200 ft.) with a diameter of 1–2 m. (say, 3–6 ft.), sometimes considerably larger. The tree may be clear of branches to a height of 30 m. (100 ft.) or more. Sawn timber is normally available in widths up to 300 mm. (12 in.), thicknesses up to 100 mm. (4 in.) and lengths mostly 4·2–4·8 m. (say, 14–16 ft.). Scantlings up to 300 mm. (12 in.) square can be obtained in lengths of 7·2 m. (24 ft.) or over. Some of the Canadian timber is supplied surfaced on four sides in nominal thicknesses of 2 in. and nominal widths up to 10 in. This is known as CLS, i.e., timber dressed to Canadian Lumber Standards, and is intended for use in constructional work, carcassing for building, etc. Douglas fir is shipped all over the world in the form of lumber, plywood and poles.

General description. Narrow-ringed wood from old trees is yellowish-brown and is sometimes marketed as yellow fir, while wide-ringed material from young trees of more rapid growth is reddish-brown (red fir). Average density is about 0·53 (33 lb./ft.^{3}), seasoned. There is a strongly marked growth-ring figure. The wood is generally straight grained. It is inclined to be resinous.

Seasoning and movement. The timber dries rapidly without much distortion or checking. FPRL kiln schedule K gives good results. Sound knots tend to split in seasoning and encased knots nearly always become loose. Movement in use is classed as small.

Strength and bending properties. Douglas fir of at least average density is strong for its weight, superior to Baltic redwood and approximately equal to pitch pine of similar grade. Narrow-ringed, low-density material is unsuitable for structural purposes. Douglas fir is also unsuitable for conventional bent work; however, clear straight-grained material is excellent for glued laminated structural bends.

Durability and preservative treatment. The heartwood is moderately durable and resistant to preservative treatment. Penetration is improved by incising.

Working and finishing properties. Douglas fir is harder to work than most commercial softwoods. The timber generally finishes well. Wide-ringed material tends to splinter and break away when cut across the grain, and the surface of planed or moulded material may show raised grain due to compression of the soft spring wood by dull cutters. Care is needed to avoid splitting in nailing. The wood takes stains and glues satisfactorily and generally gives good results with the usual finishing treatments. Resinous timber should be kiln-dried if it is to be varnished or painted.

Uses. The chief advantages of Douglas fir are its strength and the large dimensions available. It is one of the best-known timbers for heavy structural purposes, including laminated arches and roof trusses. It is also used for vats and tanks for industrial processes. Selected material is widely used for joinery. As flooring, in the form of rift-sawn (edge-grain) material, it is suitable for comparatively light traffic. In the round it is used for transmission poles of larger dimensions than can be obtained from Baltic redwood. Large quantities of Douglas fir plywood are manufactured in western Canada and USA.

Douglas Fir

Rotary cut

 Reproduced two-thirds actual size

Hemlock, Western

[Tsuga heterophylla]

Distribution and supplies. Western hemlock (*Tsuga heterophylla*) is one of the major timbers of Western Canada and the USA. Like other timber trees of the region it is a tall tree, frequently reaching a height of 45–60 m. (150–200 ft.) and a diameter of 1 m. or more (say, 3–4 ft.), though generally somewhat less. The timber is in good supply and is regularly exported, sawn to widths up to 300 mm. (12 in.), thicknesses up to 100 mm. (4 in.) and lengths mostly 4·2–4·8 m. (14–16 ft.). Some of the Canadian timber, dressed to CLS grade, is surfaced on four sides in nominal thicknesses of 2 in. and nominal widths up to 10 in. Commercial shipments may include a percentage of the closely allied species mountain hemlock (*T. mertensiana*) and true fir (*Abies* spp., see below); western hemlock grown in Britain, being the product of comparatively small trees, is inferior to the imported timber in general quality.

General description. The timber is intermediate between Douglas fir and spruce in character. It is non-resinous, nearly white to pale-brown, typically straight grained with well-marked growth rings, non-resinous and odourless when dry. Average density is about 0·51 (32 lb./ft.³), seasoned.

Seasoning and movement. Western hemlock has a high moisture content when green and seasons more slowly than Douglas fir. With care it can be dried in the air or in a kiln without much distortion. Shrinkage during seasoning is high but the timber is moderately stable in service.

Strength properties. Western hemlock is less strong than Douglas fir but stronger than spruce. In most strength properties it resembles Baltic redwood.

Durability and preservative treatment. The timber is similar to spruce in durability and is unsuitable for use in exposed situations, especially as it resists preservative treatment.

Working and finishing properties. The wood works well in all hand and machine operations with little dulling effect on tools and cutters though it is about 20 per cent harder to work than Baltic redwood. Sharp tools are essential for a clean, smooth finish. It takes nails and screws well, is less inclined than Douglas fir to split in nailing, and gives satisfactory results with stain, paint and glue.

Uses. Western hemlock is used for constructional work as an alternative to Douglas fir where the lower strength is acceptable and a decay-resistant timber is not required; also for interior woodwork, flooring and many other purposes where a fairly high-grade softwood is needed.

Other species of interest. *Eastern hemlock (*T. canadensis*) of eastern Canada and USA is a comparatively small tree, usually 0·45–0·6 m. (1½–2 ft.) in diameter. The timber is inferior to that of western hemlock, being relatively coarse textured, cross-grained, fairly difficult to season and inclined to splinter. It is used mainly for rough constructional work.*
Two species of true fir, amabilis fir (Abies amabilis) and grand fir (A. grandis), both loosely referred to as western balsam, grow in association with western hemlock and are commonly shipped with the latter as hemlock/balsam (trade name hembal). The timber is more like spruce in general character and is inferior to western hemlock for constructional work, flooring and interior woodwork. (However, tests have shown that the average strength of timber in commercial mixed consignments is high enough for it to be included in the same group, S2, as unmixed hemlock in the British Standard classification of softwoods for structural purposes (B.S. Code of Practice 112: 1967, Table 9)).

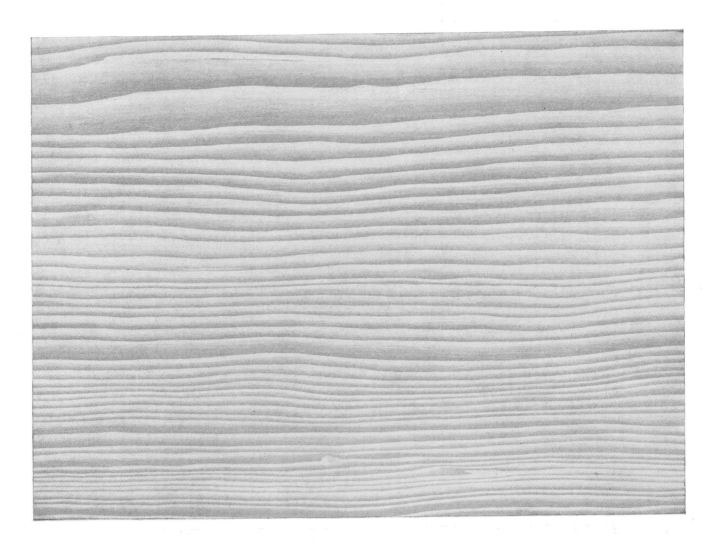

Hemlock

Quarter cut

 Reproduced actual size

Pine, Pitch or Longleaf

[Pinus palustris and allied species]

American pitch pine is the British Standard name for the denser grades of *Pinus palustris* and *P. elliottii,* as defined by the US Southern Pine Inspection Bureau; in USA, wood of this quality is known as longleaf yellow pine or simply longleaf. Material that does not meet this specification is classed as southern pine or southern yellow pine. Caribbean pitch pine is a trade name for the timber of *P. caribaea* and *P. oocarpa* of Central America and the West Indies; it is also marketed as Caribbean longleaf and as Honduras, Nicaraguan and Bahamas pitch pine, according to origin.

Distribution and supplies. American pitch pine is the common pine of the south-eastern United States. The mature tree is of excellent form, up to 30 m. (100 ft.) in height with a diameter of 0·6–0·9 m. (2–3 ft.). Formerly the timber was widely used in America, and exported in large quantities, but owing to diminishing supplies has been replaced to some extent on the export market by pitch pine shipped from Honduras and Nicaragua as baulks 6–7·5 m. (20–25 ft.) long and 300–350 mm. (12–14 in.) square and in smaller dimensions from the Bahamas.

General description. Pitch pine is typically harder and heavier than other softwoods in common use. Growth rings are strongly marked, giving the timber a characteristic appearance. The width of the rings, combined with the percentage of dense summer wood on the end grain, is used to estimate the quality of the timber for structural purposes—in effect to differentiate the dense longleaf pine or export-grade pitch pine from the remainder. Average density of the North American timber of export grade is about 0·67 (42 lb./ft.³), seasoned; Caribbean pitch pine averages about 0·70 (44 lb./ft.³). Timber from the Bahamas is comparatively narrow ringed. As the name implies, pitch pine has a high resin content.

Seasoning and movement. The timber dries fairly slowly and tends to split, check and distort. Shrinkage is moderately large but the wood is reputed to be stable when properly seasoned.

Strength properties. Pitch pine is stronger than most commercial softwoods. For structural use it is classed with Douglas fir and larch. Timber from the Caribbean area tends to be stronger and harder than that from the southern states.

Durability and preservative treatment. The heartwood is moderately durable, i.e., superior to Baltic redwood and in the same class as Douglas fir and larch. It is fairly resistant to impregnation but poles and structural timbers with a proportion of sapwood are commonly treated.

Working and finishing properties. The wood is harder to work than most commercial softwoods, being similar to Douglas fir in this respect. Well-seasoned material generally finishes cleanly though resin is sometimes troublesome. It holds nails and screws firmly, gives fairly satisfactory results with paint, varnish and other finishing treatments and glues fairly well.

Uses. Pitch pine of appropriate quality is the principal constructional timber in the southern states. Lower-grade lumber serves as a general-purpose softwood. Plantation material is largely used for pulping. In Britain pitch pine was formerly popular for purposes where its large dimensions and higher than average strength were an advantage, notably for piling, dock work and the roof timbers of public buildings; it was also traditional for church furniture, school desks and block flooring. Latterly it has assumed the position of a special-purpose timber, for example it is one of the best timbers for vats for a wide range of purposes including the manufacture of chemicals and foodstuffs. In the boat-building industry it is used for planking.

Pine, Pitch

Flat cut

Reproduced actual size

65

Pine, Red

[*Pinus resinosa*]

Distribution and supplies. Red pine is a species of comparatively minor importance as timber, found in eastern Canada and USA. The tree is commonly 23–30 m. (75–100 ft.) in height and 0·5–0·76 m. (20–30 in.) in diameter. The timber is mainly utilised locally; small quantities have been exported to Britain from Canada in much the same range of sizes as eastern Canadian spruce. In the USA it has been mixed with white pine (*Pinus strobus*) and jack pine (*P. banksiana*) for the local market.

General description. The timber closely resembles Baltic redwood. The heartwood is pale reddish-brown, resinous, distinct from the wide creamy-white sapwood. The average density is about 0·45 (28 lb./ft.³) in the seasoned condition. Growth rings are clearly marked by the contrast between the light spring wood and the dark summer wood zones. The wood is generally straight grained except in the neighbourhood of knots, which occur at fairly regular intervals.

Seasoning and movement. The timber seasons easily and uniformly without serious degrade. Shrinkage in drying is fairly high but once seasoned the movement is classed as medium. Kiln seasoning has the advantage of hardening the resin, so improving the finishing qualities.

Strength properties. Red pine is a softwood of average strength, i.e., it is stronger than white pine and about equal to Baltic redwood except that it is slightly softer.

Durability and preservative treatment. Red pine is classed as non-durable but is superior to white pine and spruce in this respect. The heartwood is moderately resistant to preservative treatment; the sapwood is permeable.

Working and finishing properties. The wood is easy to work, takes a good finish, holds nails and screws well and presents no difficulty in staining, painting and gluing.

Uses. Red pine is essentially a general-utility timber for carpentry and joinery, mainly used in house building, for interior and exterior work, and for boxes and crates. In Britain it is regarded as an alternative to Baltic redwood.

EI

Pine, Red

Quarter cut

Reproduced actual size

Pine, Yellow or White

[*Pinus strobus*]

Yellow pine is the British Standard name for the timber commonly known in Canada and the USA as white pine, eastern white pine or northern white pine.

Distribution and supplies. Although stands of this valuable timber have been so heavily cut and much of the present production is second growth, it is still one of the more important species of eastern Canada and USA. Trees are generally 28–38 m. (90–125 ft.) in height and 0·5–0·75 (20–30 in.) in diameter. Commercial production is almost entirely lumber in relatively small dimensions. Limited quantities are exported for special purposes, as noted below.

General description. Yellow pine is well known for its soft, light, straight-grained, even-textured wood. Second-growth timber, however, is inclined to be knotty and cross grained. The heartwood is pale yellowish-brown to reddish-brown, the sapwood nearly white. Average density is about 0·39 (24 lb./ft.^{3}), seasoned.

Seasoning and movement. The timber seasons easily and uniformly with little shrinkage. Movement in service is exceptionally small.

Strength properties. Yellow pine ranks low in strength compared with other commercial species of pine. It is more like spruce in this respect.

Durability and preservative treatment. The timber is classed as non-durable. The heartwood is moderately resistant to preservative treatment, the sapwood permeable.

Working and finishing properties. Yellow pine works exceptionally well, taking a smooth, satin-like finish, and is excellent for carving. It has good nailing and screwing properties and takes stain, paint and varnish.

Uses. The wood is ideal where a soft but even-textured, easily worked, stable timber is required. In Britain the high price limits its use to exacting purposes, including engineers' patterns, drawing boards, match sticks and organ building. In Canada and the USA it is used for a wider range of work, including interior woodwork, cabinet-making, boat building, toys and woodware for use in kitchens and dairies.

Other species of interest. *Two other commercial species closely allied to yellow pine are found in western North America. Western white pine (*P. monticola*) and sugar pine (*P. lambertiana*) resemble yellow pine in structure and properties and are used for similar purposes. They are obtainable in larger sizes. It is appropriate to mention also ponderosa pine (*P. ponderosa*) of British Columbia and the western United States. The quality of this timber varies widely. Mature trees have a thick, pale-yellow sapwood, soft, non-resinous and uniform in texture, resembling yellow pine and western white pine in general character and used for similar purposes. The heartwood is darker and considerably denser than the sapwood. Average density for the species is about 0·51 (32 lb./ft.^{3}), seasoned.*

Pine, Yellow

Flat cut

Reproduced actual size

Redwood, California

[Sequoia sempervirens]

Distribution and supplies. The California redwood grows to an enormous size, up to 90 m. (say, 300 ft.) or more in height and commonly 1·5–3 m. (5–10 ft.) in diameter. Lumber is available in a wide range of sizes free from defects. In America, commercial production is limited to California. The tree is grown successfully in plantations in some of the milder parts of Britain.

General description. The wood is typically soft and light, average density 0·43 (27 lb./ft.³) in the seasoned condition, resembling western red cedar in general character. It varies considerably in different parts of the tree from light cherry-red to dark reddish-brown, from fine, even-textured wood (narrow rings) to coarse-textured, wide-ringed material. It is usually straight grained but wood from near the base of the tree often has a decorative curly grain and occasional burrs yield a highly figured wood which is cut into veneers resembling thuya burr. Redwood is non-resinous and non-tainting.

Technical properties. The timber can be dried easily with little shrinkage or checking and is stable in service. It is moderately strong for its weight but less strong than the general run of constructional softwoods. California redwood is renowned for its durability, is fairly easy to work in all hand and machine operations, takes and holds nails well and gives good results with paint and the usual finishing treatments.

Uses. California redwood is largely used in America in house building for interior finish and for exterior work. Because of its durability it is commonly chosen for cooling towers, wood pipes, vats, tanks and silos, greenhouses and farm buildings. Timber grown in Britain is comparatively light in weight, soft and coarse textured, suitable for purposes where durability is the main consideration.

Other species of interest. *The giant sequoia or bigtree (*Sequoiadendron giganteum*) is found in a limited area in the mountains of California. The wood is even lighter than that of California redwood but highly durable. It is no longer of commercial importance since the trees are protected. In Britain, where it is commonly known as Wellingtonia, the tree has been extensively planted in avenues, parks and gardens. The wood from such trees is coarse and knotty.*

Redwood

Burr

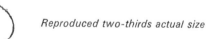

Reproduced two-thirds actual size

Spruce, Eastern

[various species of *Picea*]

The North American species of spruce provide two main types of commercial timber, Eastern spruce, of eastern Canada and the USA—comprising white spruce (*Picea glauca*), red spruce (*P. rubens*) and black spruce (*P. mariana*)—and Sitka or silver spruce (*P. sitchensis*) of British Columbia and the western United States, which is described separately. A third type, Engelmann spruce (*P. engelmannii*), from the Rocky Mountain region, is of minor importance as a world timber, its use being practically confined to the interior of the country. It resembles eastern spruce but, being a larger tree, yields a higher proportion of clear wood. Western white spruce, of Alberta and British Columbia (a variety of *P. glauca*), is also generally superior to eastern spruce in quality. In terms of annual production, spruce is Canada's most important timber.

Distribution and supplies. The distributions of the three species of Eastern spruce overlap and virtually no distinction is made between their timbers. Large quantities are exported from Canada, mainly to Britain, shipments being commonly designated by the name of the province or port, e.g., Quebec, New Brunswick, St. John, or as Maritime spruce. The trees are comparatively small, rarely more than 23 m. (75 ft.) high and 0·6 m. (2 ft.) in diameter. The timber is normally available in sizes similar to Baltic whitewood, i.e., 50–75 mm. (2–3 in.) thick, in widths up to 225 mm. (9 in.), rarely 300 mm. (12 in.), in lengths of 2·4–5·1 m. (8–17 ft.). It is mainly of building grade.

General description. Eastern spruce closely resembles Baltic whitewood (European spruce). The wood is nearly white with no visible difference between sapwood and heartwood, lustrous, fairly straight grained, without appreciable odour when dry, non-tainting and only slightly resinous. It is lighter in weight than most commercial softwoods; the seasoned timber averages about 0·42 (26 lb./ft.³) in density.

Seasoning and movement. The timber can be dried rapidly with little tendency to split or check. It is stable in service.

Strength properties. Grade for grade, eastern spruce is similar to its European counterpart, Baltic whitewood; it is of medium strength and noted for its resilience.

Durability and preservative treatment. Like other species of spruce, the timber is susceptible to fungal and insect attack and is classed as non-durable. Moreover, it is not easily treated with preservatives, even under pressure.

Working and finishing properties. The timber works very easily in all hand and machine operations and has little effect on cutting edges except where knots occur. It takes a smooth, silky finish, nails well and does not tend to split in nailing. It takes paint well and can be glued satisfactorily.

Uses. The timber is used for conventional building work where the decay hazard is slight, for light construction, especially where a clean, white appearance is desired, also for piano sound-boards, and boxes and crates, especially for foodstuffs. Poles are used for half-round ladder sides. The largest use is for pulp.

Spruce, Eastern

Flat cut

 Reproduced actual size

Spruce, Sitka

[*Picea sitchensis*]

Distribution and supplies. The Sitka spruce or silver spruce of British Columbia and the western United States is important as a source of high-grade timber in large dimensions. It is a large tree, commonly 45–60 m. (say, 150–200 ft.) in height and 1–1·8 m. (3–6 ft.) in diameter. Selected timber as shipped to Britain is available in widths of 100–300 mm. (4–12 in.) and thicknesses of 25–100 mm. (1–4 in.); lengths are normally 2·4–7·2 m. (8–24 ft.), occasionally longer.
Sitka spruce is the most widely planted conifer in Britain. Its great advantage is its rapid growth rate under a wide range of conditions. Most of the timber produced has come from comparatively young trees; it tends to be coarse and knotty, spiral grained and deficient in strength. Trees that are allowed to grow on to 80 years of age or more, however, should yield a substantial proportion of timber similar to eastern Canadian spruce and Baltic whitewood.

General description. Sitka differs from other species of spruce in its light pinkish-brown heartwood. The export-quality timber, cut from the outer portions of mature trees, is of moderate to slow growth, with a fine, silky texture, mostly straight grained and remarkably free from defects. The average density in the seasoned condition is about 0·43 (27 lb./ft.^{3}). Timber from nearer the centre of the tree is typically of coarser texture with a tendency to spiral grain.

Seasoning and movement. The timber dries fairly rapidly. Where spiral grain is present some warping and splitting is likely to occur. FPRL kiln schedule J is recommended. The wood holds its place well when manufactured.

Strength properties. Sitka spruce has exceptionally high strength properties for its weight. Although some 10 per cent lighter than Baltic redwood and red pine, it is about 25 per cent stiffer and equal to them in bending strength and resistance to splitting.

Durability and preservative treatment. Like other species of spruce, Sitka is susceptible to insect and fungal attack and is classed as non-durable. It is resistant to pressure treatment but green timber can be impregnated by a diffusion process.

Working and finishing properties. The timber works easily in all hand and machine operations, with little dulling effect on cutting edges, and takes a smooth, silky finish provided that sharp tools are used. It takes nails and screws well, gives good results with the usual finishing treatments, and can be glued satisfactorily.

Uses. By virtue of its comparatively high strength, combined with its freedom from defects and the large dimensions in which it is available, Sitka spruce assumed great importance during the first world war for aeroplane construction. It is still used for light aircraft such as gliders and is a standard timber in the boat building industry, for masts and spars, for the hulls of racing eights, yachts and dinghies and for oars and paddles. Other uses include piano sound-boards and in organ building. The lower-grade timber is used in North America for the same purposes as the other species of spruce. Some timber from the relatively small trees grown in Britain is used for boxes, packing cases and rough construction but most of it goes for pulping and as raw material for fibreboard, chipboard and wood-wool.

Spruce, Sitka

Flat cut

Reproduced actual size

Quarter cut

South American Timbers

[*including Central America & the West Indies*]

HARDWOODS

Andiroba or Crabwood

[Carapa guianensis]

Andiroba (the Brazilian name) or crabwood (as it is known in Guyana) is related to the mahoganies (*Swietenia* and *Khaya*) and is sometimes marketed as Demerara mahogany or Surinam mahogany, though it is not generally accepted as a mahogany on the world market. Because of the variation in the character of the wood it has been suggested that the name andiroba should be used for the finer-textured, denser material and the name crabwood for the coarser-textured wood of medium density.

Distribution and supplies. On the mainland of South America this species is found in Brazil, the Guianas, Venezuela, Colombia and possibly Peru, and extends to the West Indian islands and through Central America as far as British Honduras. It attains a large size, being commonly more than 30 m. (100 ft.) in height and 1 m. or more (say, 3–4 ft.) in diameter. It has been exported to Europe and the USA from Brazil, Guyana and Surinam, where it is reported to be very common.

General description. Superficially the timber resembles plain mahogany; it tends to be somewhat darker in colour and lacks the natural lustre of true mahogany. It is also appreciably denser, averaging about 0·64 (40 lb./ft.^{3}), seasoned. The grain is typically straight, though figured material is sometimes found.

Seasoning and movement. The timber dries rather slowly, tending to split and distort. FPRL kiln schedule C has given satisfactory results. Dimensional movement in service is small though the wood is less stable than mahogany.

Strength and bending properties. Appreciably harder and stronger than Central American mahogany. Small-scale steam-bending tests indicate that it cannot be bent without buckling.

Durability and preservative treatment. It is moderately resistant to decay. Logs are liable to be severely attacked by pinhole-borer beetles. No information is available about preservative treatment.

Working and finishing properties. The timber is rated 25 per cent harder to cut than Central American mahogany. When the grain is interlocked the surface is likely to tear in planing unless the cutting angle is adjusted; an angle of 15° is recommended. It tends to split when nailed, gives good results with staining and the usual finishing treatments and is believed to take glue satisfactorily.

Uses. Andiroba or crabwood has been used as a substitute for mahogany for furniture and similar purposes and locally for all kinds of construction work where a high resistance to decay is not required.

Andiroba

Flat cut

Reproduced actual size

Balsa

[Ochroma pyramidale]

Distribution and supplies. Balsa is widely distributed in tropical America. The main source of supply is plantations in Ecuador and it is also grown successfully in Ceylon, Java and the Caribbean region. The tree grows extremely fast, attaining a height of 18–27 m. (60–90 ft.) and a diameter of 0·6–0·9 m. (2–3 ft.) in 6–10 years, when it is ready for cutting. The wood is normally shipped in the form of lumber, in random lengths averaging less than 1·5 m. (5 ft.) and widths averaging about 125 mm. (5 in.).

General description. Balsa is the lightest commercial timber. The density varies widely, depending on the age of the tree and conditions of growth. Commercial material normally has a density range of 0·1–0·26 (6–16 lb./ft.^{3}), seasoned. It consists mainly of sapwood, which is whitish or oatmeal-coloured, sometimes with a yellowish or pinkish hue. It has an even texture and is moderately firm for its weight, soft and velvety to the touch, with a silky lustre.

Seasoning and movement. Balsa must be converted and dried immediately after felling to obviate fungal discoloration and decay. Once seasoned it is fairly stable and is classed as having small movement.

Strength and bending properties. The strength varies directly with density and, where strength is important, material should be selected on a density basis with reference to published strength figures. As a rough guide it can be taken that commercial balsa of average density has from one-half to one-third the strength of spruce. Balsa is unsuitable for solid bends since it cannot be bent without buckling, but can be used for bent members of composite construction.

Durability and preservative treatment. Under damp conditions balsa is highly susceptible to attack by fungi and wood-destroying insects unless adequately protected by painting or preservative treatment. The sapwood is readily permeable.

Working and finishing properties. The wood is easily worked to a smooth, clean finish provided that very sharp, thin-edged tools are used. It is too soft to hold nails or screws firmly but can be glued satisfactorily.

Uses. Balsa is well known as the ideal material for making models, properties for theatrical and film productions and many other purposes where a light, soft yet firm material is required. It became famous during the second world war for its use in "sandwich" construction, particularly for aircraft. On account of its low thermal conductivity it is used for insulation purposes, as in refrigerators and cold stores. Other uses include protective packing for fragile goods and delicate instruments, and in life-saving rafts and floats. Its superior strength gives it an advantage over expanded polystyrene, granulated cork and slag-wool.

Balsa

Flat cut

Reproduced actual size

Balsamo

[Myroxylon balsamum]

The trade name balsamo is in general use for this timber in Latin America. In Brazil it is also known as cabreuva, cabreuva vermelha and oleo vermelho.

Distribution and supplies. This is a medium-sized tree, usually 15–18 m. (50–60 ft.) high but often taller and 0·45–0·75 m. (say, 18–30 in.) in diameter. It is widely distributed in tropical America, from southern Mexico to Argentina, but not in the Amazon basin, and it is possible that the Argentine timber, although very similar to that from elsewhere, should be regarded as a separate species. In the past the tree has been of more importance as a source of balsam, notably from Salvador, than for its timber and it has been planted as a balsam producer elsewhere in the tropics; up to now, only small quantities of the timber have been available, almost entirely from Brazil.

General description. The heartwood is a deep reddish-brown, sometimes with a faint purplish hue; it has a fairly uniform appearance on flat-cut surfaces and with a moderately fine texture has a superficial resemblance to plain Cuban mahogany. When quartered, it shows a prominent, narrow stripe figure due to the markedly interlocked grain. It is a very heavy wood, density about 1·2 (64 lb./ft.^{3}), seasoned, with a pleasant spicy scent.

Technical properties. As for so many tropical American timbers, its technical properties are still imperfectly known. It is hard, tough and strong; little is known about its seasoning properties but small heartwood specimens have retained their shape well under laboratory conditions and the shrinkage on drying can be rated as moderately low. It has been reported as moderately difficult to work and, though it can be finished very smoothly, particular care is needed with quartered stock having a deeply interlocked grain; it is non-siliceous. The heartwood has a reputation for high natural durability.

Uses. An attractive, if somewhat plain wood, particularly on flat-cut surfaces, its use is likely to be limited by its weight. It is most suitable for heavy, durable outdoor construction and might find acceptance for some external joinery, such as thresholds, sills, etc. With its fine, even texture, it should make a hard-wearing floor. As veneer it has a plain appearance when flat cut and has a narrow stripe figure when quartered.

82

Balsamo

Flat cut

 Reproduced actual size

Basralocus or Angélique

[Dicorynia guianensis]

The trade name basralocus refers to timber from Surinam. Timber from French Guiana is known as angélique or teck de la Guyane. This tree was formerly classified as *Dicorynia paraensis* but that name is now restricted to the closely allied Brazilian species found in the Amazon region.

Distribution and supplies. This timber is reported to be in good supply in Surinam and French Guiana. It is exported in the form of round logs and sawn piles, averaging 250 mm. (10 in.) square (max. 400 mm. or 16 in.), in lengths up to 10 m. (33 ft.) or more, and as lumber 25–100 mm. (1–4 in.) thick, averaging 200 mm. (8 in.) wide (max. 450 mm. or 18 in.), in lengths of 4·2 m. (say, 14 ft.) and up, average about 5 m. (say, 16 ft.). Quarter-sawn material for decking is also available.

General description. The heartwood is of plain appearance, pinkish-brown when freshly cut, darkening to reddish-brown or purplish-brown. The grain is straight or slightly interlocked (quarter-sawn material is more or less striped due to the interlocked grain); the texture medium. The average density of well-seasoned timber is about 0·72 (45 lb./ft.^{3}), i.e., about the same as oak.

Seasoning. Attempts to kiln season freshly sawn, green material resulted in serious degrade due to collapse, distortion, splitting and case-hardening. Air drying is to be preferred; alternatively a combination of air and kiln seasoning, using a normal hardwood kiln schedule.

Strength properties. The results of limited laboratory tests show that the timber compares favourably with teak, though it splits readily.

Durability. Basralocus is known to be highly resistant to marine borers in tropical and temperate waters (this is attributed to the presence of silica particles in the wood) and is reputed to be resistant to termites. Laboratory tests have shown that it is also resistant to fungal decay. It is very durable.

Working and finishing properties. The silica content sometimes makes the wood difficult to saw and machine. As far as possible it should be sawn and worked in the unseasoned condition to minimise the blunting effect. For working seasoned material, carbide-tipped tools are essential and under these conditions a smooth finish is obtained. Gluing is satisfactory.

Uses. Because of its high rating for strength and durability, its moderate density and the large dimensions available, this timber is particularly suitable for harbour works, bridges, piers, wharves and similar purposes. Quarter-sawn material should be specified for decking. In the USA it has also been used for flooring.

Basralocus

Flat cut

  Reproduced actual size

Boxwood, Maracaibo or West Indian

[Gossypiospermum praecox]

Though botanically unrelated to the original boxwood of Europe and Asia Minor (*Buxus sempervirens*), this species is universally accepted as a commercial boxwood.

Distribution and supplies. The timber is exported from the Lake Maracaibo region of Venezuela, where it is known as zapatero, and from Colombia. It is also found in Cuba and the Dominican Republic. It is a small- to medium-sized tree furnishing logs upwards of 200 mm. (8 in.) in diameter and 2·4–3·6 m. (8–12 ft.) in length, i.e., considerably larger and of better shape than European boxwood. It is one of the most important boxwoods of commerce.

General description. The colour varies from nearly white to clear light-yellow, with little or no difference between heartwood and sapwood, though blue stain may develop in storage. The texture is extremely fine and even and the grain usually straight. The density is slightly less than that of European boxwood, 0·80–0·90 (50–56 lb./ft.^{3}) in the seasoned condition.

Technical properties. The wood differs from European boxwood in being slightly less hard and dense; it also splits more readily. In other respects it is very similar, being easy to carve and turn, taking a very smooth, clean finish from the tool.

Uses. The straight grain and the comparatively large sizes available make Maracaibo boxwood specially suitable for draughtsmen's rulers and scales, for which it has largely replaced European boxwood. It is also used for small articles of turnery, for bushes and bearings in textile machinery, and in musical instruments.

Boxwood, Maracaibo

Flat cut

 Reproduced actual size

Boxwood, San Domingo

[Phyllostylon brasiliensis]

Distribution and supplies. As the trade name implies, this species is common in the Dominican Republic, which is the main source of supply of the timber for the export market. It is also found in Cuba and is widely distributed on the mainland from Mexico to northern Argentina. It has entered Britain in the form of logs, 150–200 mm. (6–8 in.) in diameter and 2·4–3·6 m. (8–12 ft.) in length.

General description. San Domingo boxwood closely resembles European boxwood in colour, grain and texture. It may be distinguished from all other commercial boxwoods by the chalky white deposits in the pores. The recorded density is about 0·95 (59 lb./ft.^{3}) in the dry condition.

Technical properties. Knowledge of the technical properties of the wood is limited to reports based on industrial experience. It is rated harder than Maracaibo boxwood, probably similar to European boxwood in this respect. It appears to be satisfactory from the point of view of working and finishing.

Uses. This timber was introduced to the USA and British markets as a substitute for Maracaibo boxwood when the latter was in short supply. It was considered satisfactory though not good enough for the best grade of rulers and shuttles for weaving silk and fine cotton fabrics. It has the advantage of being obtainable in fairly large dimensions and is said to be the best variety of boxwood now available for the heads of croquet mallets.

Boxwood, San Domingo

Flat cut

  Reproduced actual size

Cedar, Central American

[Cedrela odorata]

In Europe and North America the name cedar generally refers to one of a number of softwoods (coniferous timbers) with a cedar-like fragrance. The name also applies to various species of *Cedrela* yielding a light hardwood. The principal commercial species is *C. odorata* (*C. mexicana*) of Central America and the West Indies, commonly known as cigar-box or Spanish cedar, or as Honduras, Mexican, Nicaraguan, etc. The principal trade name in Latin America is cedro.

Distribution and supplies. The natural range covers the southern half of Mexico, the whole of Central America and the West Indies. The tree varies considerably in size and form, reaching 30 m. (100 ft.) or more in height and 0·6–1·2 m. (2–4 ft.) in diameter above the buttresses. The timber is in good supply locally. It is usually shipped as square-edged lumber, 100 mm. (4 in.) and up wide, 25–75 mm. (1–3 in.) thick, in lengths averaging about 3 m. (10 ft.).

General description. Central American cedar resembles American mahogany but is softer and coarser. The wood varies appreciably, timber of vigorous growth tending to be paler and lighter in weight than that from more slowly grown trees. Average density is about 0·48 (30 lb./ft.^{3}) when dry, i.e., little heavier than gaboon or okoumé. Colour varies from a pale to medium red-brown but darkens on exposure; the grain is usually straight. Its fragrant scent, particularly marked when freshly surfaced, helps to distinguish cedar from mahogany; also some pieces have an oily exudation which dries to a sticky surface.

Seasoning and movement. Cedar kiln-dries rapidly and well but with a tendency to distort and collapse. Shrinkage on drying is a little greater than that of American mahogany but movement in service is small.

Strength and bending properties. A light wood and relatively variable in weight, it has correspondingly low and variable strength properties, somewhat less than those of American mahogany, especially in hardness, compression parallel to the grain and shear. It has fairly good steam-bending properties and is suitable for making bends of moderate radius of curvature.

Durability and preservative treatment. Cedar is durable under tropical conditions, being resistant to fungal and insect attack, including termites. The heartwood resists pressure treatment.

Working and finishing properties. The wood works easily with hand and machine tools provided that tools are kept sharp. Its most troublesome feature is the gum which may build up on cutters and adhere to machine tables and feed rollers. The gum may also cause trouble if surfaces are polished. The wood can be screwed, nailed, glued and varnished satisfactorily, and can be rotary peeled and sliced to show an attractive decorative surface.

Uses. By virtue of its durability, excellent working qualities and appearance, cedar is perhaps the most important local timber for domestic use in tropical America. It serves for all kinds of building work, other than heavy construction, and for joinery and cabinet work. In Europe and North America it is best known for its use in cigar boxes. It is a favourite timber for the hulls of light racing boats.

Other species of interest. *Other closely allied species are found in tropical South America.*

Cedar

Flat cut

   Reproduced actual size

Cocuswood

[Brya ebenus]

Cocuswood is also known as brown ebony, green ebony and Jamaican ebony and as granadillo, a name also applied to partridgewood or maracaibo from Venezuela.

Distribution and supplies. This is a small tree, rarely more than 8 m. (say, 25 ft.) tall and 200 mm. (8 in.) in diameter, found in Jamaica and Cuba. The wood has long been exported in small quantities in the form of logs, usually 1·2–2·4 m. (4–8 ft.) long and 75–150 mm. (3–6 in.) in diameter. They are shipped entire to protect the heartwood from checking and splitting. In recent years supplies have been difficult to obtain.

General description. The general colour of the heartwood is dark chocolate-brown to nearly black, variegated or finely striped, contrasting sharply with the yellowish sapwood. It is extremely dense, about 1·2 (75 lb./ft.^{3}), with a fine, uniform texture and a natural lustre due to the oily nature of the wood.

Technical properties. The wood requires care in seasoning, but is reported to hold its place well when manufactured. It is tough and strong, but not unduly difficult to work, taking a smooth, waxy finish.

Uses. Cocuswood has been used for making musical instruments, particularly flutes, clarinets and oboes, but has been largely superseded, in Britain, by African blackwood. Its handsome appearance and excellent turning properties make it suitable for small articles of turnery.

Cocuswood

Flat cut

Reproduced actual size

Freijo

[Cordia goeldiana]

Distribution and supplies. Freijo is a well-known timber of the Brazilian Amazon. The tree is of medium size, up to about 30 m. (100 ft.) in height and 0·6–0·9 m. (2–3 ft.) in diameter. The timber has been exported to Europe and the USA in small quantities from time to time but is of minor commercial importance outside Brazil.

General description. Freijo has some resemblance to teak in colour, grain and texture and has, in fact, been marketed under the name of Brazilian teak. The yellow-brown heartwood is sometimes marked with darker streaks which enhance its appearance. It is somewhat lighter than teak, average density about 0·61 (38 lb./ft.³) in the seasoned condition.

Technical properties. The timber can be dried readily without much splitting or distortion and has the reputation of being stable in service. The results of laboratory tests indicate that it is about as strong as teak in most respects but superior in toughness. It is classed as durable but is probably not equal to teak in this respect. It works easily, taking a clean finish.

Uses. Freijo is used in Brazil for a wide range of purposes, including high-class furniture and joinery, boat building and vehicle body building. It is an attractive timber deserving greater consideration than it has received on the world market.

Other species of interest. *There are several other species of* Cordia *in tropical and temperate South America, furnishing high-quality timbers resembling freijo in general character and used for similar purposes. The range of C.* alliodora *extends from the West Indies and Central America to Brazil. The timber is unusually variable in colour and density and is variously known as laurel negro, laurel blanco, laurel amarillo, etc., salmwood (British Honduras) and cyp or cypre (Trinidad), among other names. In southern Brazil and Argentina the principal species is C.* trichotoma, *known as louro (Brazil), loro or peterebi (Argentina).*

94

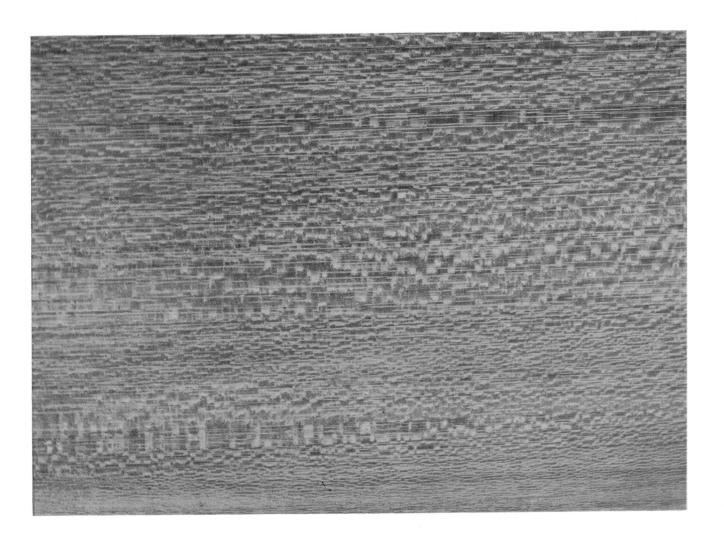

Freijo

Quarter cut

Reproduced actual size

Gonçalo Alves

[Astronium fraxinifolium and *A. graveolens]*

This timber is sometimes known as zebrawood, a name applied to several unrelated species with light and dark markings. In the USA it has been marketed as kingwood and tigerwood.

Distribution and supplies. Both species have a wide distribution, from Mexico and Central America to Ecuador, Colombia, Venezuela and Brazil. Commercial shipments are obtained mainly from eastern Brazil where the trade name gonçalo alves applies. The trees are of medium size, commonly 23 m. (75 ft.) in height and 0·6–0·9 m. (2–3 ft.) in diameter, yielding clear, straight, sound cylindrical logs.

General description. The heartwood has a striking appearance, brown to deep mahogany red-brown with conspicuous dark-brown or black, fairly irregular markings. The grain is straight to interlocked and occasionally slightly wavy, sometimes giving rise to a stripe or fiddle-back figure which adds to the decorative appearance; texture is moderately fine and even. Gonçalo alves is a heavy wood, density about 0·95 (59 lb./ft.^{3}), seasoned, similar in weight to Rhodesian teak.

Seasoning and movement. The timber air seasons moderately quickly, but care is needed to avoid excessive checking and warping; movement data are not available but shrinkage on drying is rated as relatively low.

Strength properties. Strength figures for gonçalo alves, though high, are below the average of other timbers of comparable weight, particularly in bending, compression, hardness and toughness.

Durability. The timber has a high reputation for durability, and laboratory tests carried out in the USA have confirmed that it is in the highest durability class when exposed to fungal attack.

Working and finishing properties. Reports on the working properties of gonçalo alves vary; it has been described as fairly easy to work, despite its high density, and to finish smoothly, though it is likely that where irregular grain is present, difficulty may be experienced in obtaining a satisfactory finish; it is said to turn and carve well and to take a high natural polish. The wood can be cut to produce highly decorative veneer but is reported to present some difficulty in gluing.

Uses. Although often highly figured, its weight limits the use of gonçalo alves as solid timber. It is of interest mainly as a decorative veneer, for inlays in high-class furniture and cabinet work. In the solid it might find acceptance for brush backs, knife handles and similar purposes where decorative woods, such as macassar ebony and rosewood, are normally used. As a flooring timber it might be expected to have a high resistance to wear, though for domestic purposes it is somewhat dark.

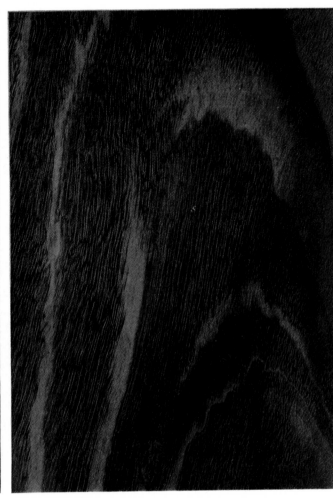

Goncalo Alves

Quarter cut

Reproduced actual size

Flat cut

Greenheart

[Ocotea rodiaei]

Distribution and supplies. Greenheart is essentially a tree of Guyana, where it is available in large quantities despite heavy logging for export for nearly 200 years. Limited quantities occur in Surinam and Brazil. It is a fine tree up to 40 m. (130 ft.) high with a long, straight cylindrical bole, commonly 15–24 m. (50–80 ft.) in length and 0·4–0·6 m. (16–24 in.) in diameter. It is shipped mostly as hewn baulks, squared to 300–400 mm. (12–16 in.), up to 12 m. (40 ft.) in length, but exceptional squares of 600 mm. (24 in.) and over 18 m. (60 ft.) long are available.

General description. Greenheart is a hard, very heavy, moderately fine-textured wood, remarkably free from knots and other defects. It has a distinctive pale to dark olive-green heartwood, often with darker, brown or black markings. The sapwood is pale, not always well defined, and about 50 mm. (2 in.) wide. The grain is straight or slightly interlocked. With an average density of about 1·03 (64 lb./ft.^{3}), seasoned, greenheart is one of the heaviest timbers in commercial use. Unseasoned, as it is generally used, the density is about 1·3 (80 lb./ft.^{3}).

Seasoning and movement. The timber seasons very slowly and in large dimensions there may be considerable degrade due to checking and splitting. FPRL kiln schedule B is recommended. However, greenheart is commonly used in baulk sizes in wet situations and the need to dry such timber does not arise. When dry, the timber is rated as having a medium movement in service.

Strength and bending properties. Greenheart is exceptionally strong for its weight. It is about 50 per cent heavier than English oak but almost twice as resistant to shock and more than twice as strong in bending, compression and stiffness. It is classed as moderately good for steam bending.

Durability and preservative treatment. Greenheart is noted for its durability, being resistant to fungi and insects, including dry-wood termites, and marine borers in salt water, though there are records of its being attacked by borers in fresh and brackish water. It is extremely resistant to preservative treatment, even under pressure.

Working and finishing properties. Greenheart presents difficulty in working with both hand and machine tools. For ripsawing, saws with 66 teeth and a 15° hook are recommended. In planing, sharp cutters with a 20° cutting angle give a good finish, but the wood has marked blunting effect and with dulled cutters the finish tends to be torn or fibrous. End-grain working requires care because the wood tends to break away at the exit of the tool. It is necessary to pre-bore for screws to avoid splitting. Greenheart produces a fine dust in machining, causing nasal irritation to some operators.

Uses. The wood has outstanding strength and durability which, combined with its availability in very large sizes, have made it world famous as a structural timber for piling, piers, dock and harbour work and lock gates. It has been used for pier decking and handrails, for industrial flooring and in the engineering industry as bearers for engines; also in the chemical industry for vats, for agitators in vats, and for filter presses. Greenheart is a standard timber for fishing rods and is also used in the sports goods industry for the shafts of rackets and for laminated archery bows.

Greenheart

Flat cut

 Reproduced actual size

Imbuya or Embuia

[Phoebe porosa]

Imbuya or embuia is the Brazilian name. The timber is also known as Brazilian walnut.

Distribution and supplies. An important timber tree in southern Brazil, where it attains a height of 40 m. (130 ft.) and a diameter of about 1·8 m. (6 ft.). The timber has been shipped to Europe and the USA but supplies for the export market are limited because of the local demand.

General description. Imbuya is variable in colour, from yellowish-brown to chocolate-brown, and may be plain or variegated. The grain may be straight, curly or wavy. The wood is considered sufficiently similar to walnut in colour, grain and texture to justify the trade name of Brazilian walnut. The average density is about 0·64 (40 lb./ft.^{3}) in the seasoned condition, i.e., about the same as European and American black walnut.

Technical properties. The timber appears to present no difficulty in seasoning and holds its place well when manufactured. It is reported to be fairly easy to work, taking a high polish, and is resistant to decay and insect attack.

Uses. In the Sao Paulo district of Brazil, imbuya is one of the more important woods for high-grade flooring, furniture and joinery and for plywood. It is said that material can be selected for colour to match any kind of walnut. It has the advantage of being obtainable in large dimensions. Figured material is sliced into decorative veneer.

Imbuya

Quarter cut

  Reproduced actual size

Kingwood

[Dalbergia cearensis]

Distribution and supplies. Kingwood is derived from a small tree growing in the dry country of Ceara, Brazil, The timber is exported in small quantities in the form of hewn logs, 1–2 m. (say, 3–6 ft.) long and 75–200 mm. (3–8 in.) in diameter, free of sapwood.

General description. Kingwood is sometimes classed as a variety of rosewood, to which it is closely related botanically, but it is sufficiently dissimilar to merit its distinctive name. The heartwood is brown with fine stripes of black or deep-violet, the pattern of striping being more regular than in Brazilian rosewood, and with more contrast. It is also appreciably denser than rosewood, average about 1·2 (75 lb./ft.³) in the seasoned condition, and of finer texture.

Technical properties. The wood is generally similar to Brazilian rosewood in technical properties but is harder and stronger. It works fairly well with sharp tools, taking a high natural polish and holds its place well when manufactured.

Uses. Kingwood has long been known to the cabinet-makers of Europe and America. Because of the small sizes available it has been used mainly for inlays, marquetry and fancy turnery. Inlaid borders of tables and cabinets in the French style are frequently of kingwood (the French name is bois de violette).

Kingwood

Flat cut

Reproduced two-thirds actual size

Lignum Vitae

[principally *Guaiacum officinale*]

Distribution and supplies. Of several species of *Guaiacum* in the tropical American region, *G. officinale* is the principal source of commercial lignum vitae. It is a small tree growing to a height of 9 m. or so (say, 30 ft.) and a diameter of 250–300 mm. (10–12 in.), occasionally much larger. Supplies originate mainly from Cuba, Jamaica, the Dominican Republic and Puerto Rico and it is known to occur also in Venezuela, Colombia, Panama and Honduras. The timber is shipped all over the world, usually as logs up to 3 m. (10 ft.) long and 75–100 mm. (3–20 in.) in diameter, characterised by a narrow ring of sapwood and known to the trade as thin-sap lignum vitae. *G. sanctum* from the Bahamas comes in smaller sizes, with a larger proportion of sapwood, and is known as thick-sap lignum vitae. Nicaragua and Mexico also contribute to world supplies.

General description. A highly distinctive timber, characterised by its great weight and oily nature. The heartwood is a peculiar dark greenish-brown or nearly black, sharply differentiated from the yellowish sapwood. The grain is closely interlocked and the texture extremely fine and even. One of the heaviest woods known, the density is about 1·23 (77 lb./ft.^{3}).

Technical properties. The wood dries very slowly; logs should be stored in a cool, shady place to avoid excessive splitting. It is one of the hardest woods known, being more than three times as hard as oak, as measured by its resistance to indentation. However, it can be split fairly easily in the tangential plane. The heartwood is practically immune to fungal and insect attack. It is difficult to work, although the dulling effect on cutting edges is not excessive owing to the oily nature of the wood. It is excellent for turning.

Uses. The exceptional hardness of lignum vitae, combined with its self-lubricating qualities due to the resin content, make it specially suitable where a high resistance to wear is required. Probably the most important use is for lining the stern tubes of ships' propeller shafts. Other typical industrial uses are for bearings, rollers for conveyors, pulleys and mallet heads. It is the only timber considered suitable for the 'woods' used in the game of bowls.

Other species of interest. *Verawood or Maracaibo lignum vitae (Bulnesia arborea), of Venezuela, is botanically related to true lignum vitae and resembles it in appearance and technical properties. It is utilised for the same purposes but is considered to be inferior for bearings.*

Lignum Vitae

Flat cut

  Reproduced actual size

Louro, Red

[Ocotea rubra]

Louro vermelho (red louro) is the Brazilian name. Other trade names are determa (Guyana) and wana (Surinam).

Distribution and supplies. This species is widely distributed in the Guianas and the Brazilian Amazon. It is a tall tree with a straight cylindrical trunk, 12–21 m. (40–70 ft.) long and 0·9–1 m. (say, 36–40 in.) in diameter. The timber is available for export in the form of lumber and as logs for conversion to veneer.

General description. A light reddish-brown wood with a golden lustre and a pleasing appearance, resembling mahogany in colour, grain and texture. The average density is slightly greater than the general run of African mahogany, about 0·62 (39 lb./ft.³) in the seasoned condition.

Seasoning and movement. The lumber seasons fairly well with a slight tendency to warp and check and is reported to stand well on exposure to the weather.

Strength properties. Laboratory tests on limited material indicate that louro is slightly inferior to Central American mahogany in strength.

Durability. The timber is reported to be highly resistant to insects and marine borers under tropical conditions and is classed as durable.

Working and finishing properties. Louro gives excellent results under normal conditions of machining provided that cutters are kept sharp. It needs careful filling before polishing. Gluing is satisfactory.

Uses. Louro is used locally for furniture and joinery, boat planking, motor body building and railway coaches. It has been used in Europe for decorative veneer and to a limited extent as an alternative to mahogany.

Other species of interest. *Louro inamui (O. barcellensis) of Brazil has been exported in small quantities. It resembles red louro in technical properties and has been used for similar purposes. It is distinguished by its golden-brown colour and fragrant smell.*

Louro

Flat cut

Reproduced two-thirds actual size

Mahogany, Central American

[principally *Swietenia macrophylla*]

Mahogany from Central America is known as Honduras, Peruvian, Tabasco, etc., according to origin, or simply as American mahogany. The commercial timber is mainly the product of *Swietenia macrophylla*, but other imperfectly known species of *Swietenia* may contribute to supplies.

Distribution and supplies. The distribution of *Swietenia* on the mainland extends from southern Mexico through Central America to Colombia, Venezuela, and the upper basin of the Amazon in eastern Peru, Brazil and Bolivia. Mexico, Honduras and Peru are among the more important producing countries. The tree typically has a straight cylindrical bole, 1·2–1·8 m. (4–6 ft.) in diameter above the buttresses and clear of branches to a height of 12–18 m. (40–60 ft.). The timber is commonly available as square-edged lumber in a wide range of sizes, up to 100 mm. (4 in.) thick, 75–450 mm. (3–18 in.) wide and 1–5·4 m. (say, 3–18 ft.) long, and as plain and decorative veneer.

General description. The quality of the commercial timber, particularly the density, hardness and colour, varies greatly with the locality. The recorded range in density is 0·40–0·85 (25–53 lb./ft.^{3}), average about 0.55 (34 lb./ft.^{3}), seasoned. The colour is to some extent correlated with the density; it varies from yellowish-brown to reddish-brown when freshly cut, darkening to a deep reddish-brown shade, practically indistinguishable from West Indian mahogany, though it is inclined to fade in strong sunlight. The texture is usually finer than that of African mahogany. A large proportion of the timber is straight grained and of plain appearance but there is a tendency to interlocked grain and other irregularities which produce a variety of figure—fiddle-back, blister, stripe or roe, curl, mottle, etc.—and the wood has a natural lustre which further enhances its appearance. When dry, it has no distinctive odour or taste.

Seasoning and movement. Mahogany dries fairly rapidly with little tendency to check or distort. FPRL kiln schedule F is recommended. Despite a tendency to interlocked grain, the wood is exceptionally stable; dimensional movement of the seasoned timber in service is small.

Strength and bending properties. The strength properties of mahogany are high for its weight, especially its resistance to bending, its stiffness and its compressive strength along the grain. In these respects, it is almost equal to European oak, though some 25 per cent lighter. It is inferior to oak in its resistance to splitting, in hardness and resistance to shock. Results of tests on a small scale indicate that it is moderately good for steam bending, probably better than African mahogany.

Durability and preservative treatment. Mahogany is not readily attacked by fungi and is classed as durable. Logs are liable to be damaged by pinhole borers. In sea water, where *Teredo* is present, the timber may be heavily infested if submerged for long. It is not amenable to preservative treatment.

Working and finishing properties. The timber has excellent working and finishing properties, and is considered superior to African mahogany in this respect.

[*continued on page 110*]

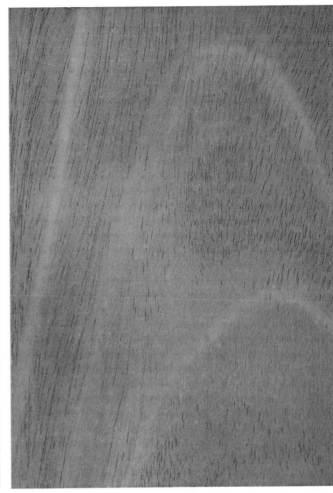

Mahogany

Quarter cut

Reproduced actual size

Flat cut

Mahogany [*continued from page 108*]

Sharp tools are essential with 'woolly' material and with highly figured wood. It has good nailing and screwing properties and can be glued satisfactorily.

Uses. Mahogany is one of the world's finest cabinet timbers. Its popularity is due to its combination of excellent working and finishing properties, stability and handsome appearance. For mass-production furniture it has been largely replaced by the less expensive and more plentiful African mahogany, but is preferred for the highest class of furniture and joinery and for reproductions. The same applies to its use in boat building and shipbuilding. Its outstanding technical qualities make it particularly suitable for precision woodwork such as engineers' patterns, instrument cases, printers' blocks and parts of musical instruments. For these purposes, plain, straight-grained material is used.

Other species of interest. *The natural range of S. mahagoni, the original mahogany of commerce, covers the West Indian islands, with the exception of Trinidad and Tobago, and southern Florida. The timber was first shipped to England and North America on a commercial scale about 1700. It established itself on both sides of the Atlantic as the premier cabinet timber of the time and became known as Spanish mahogany (in reference to the former Spanish colonies), alternatively Jamaican, San Domingo, Cuban mahogany, etc., according to origin. It was the principal timber used for many masterpieces of design and craftsmanship in the Georgian period. Later, when large, high-quality logs became scarce, it was gradually replaced by the closely allied mahogany of Central America and eventually ceased to figure in the world market, though small stocks are still carried by some timber merchants and furniture manufacturers. It may be supposed that material obtained by breaking down furniture and panelling of the Victorian era will continue to supply the limited demand for some time to come.*
West Indian mahogany is typically denser and finer-textured than Central American and African mahogany, the average density being about 0·72 (45 lb./ft.³). The characteristic colour is deep reddish-brown. The remarkably handsome appearance of the wood, especially in the form of panelling and furniture presenting a broad surface, is enhanced by a natural lustre and by the highly ornamental character of figured material due to irregularities of the grain. The technical properties are those of a dense grade of the Central American variety.
Nowadays, West Indian mahogany is rarely used except for repairs and reproductions. Apart from questions of supply and fashion, the softer mahoganies of Central America and West Africa are preferred for modern high-speed production methods.

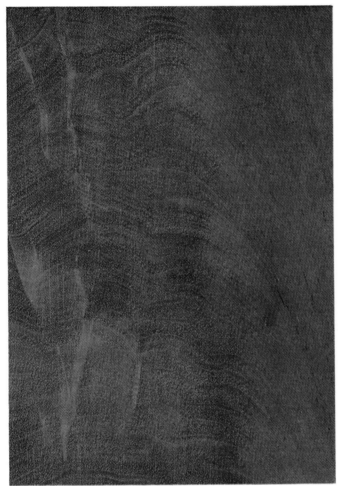

Mahogany

Curl

Reproduced actual size

Flat cut

Mora

[Mora excelsa]

Distribution and supplies. Mora is an important timber in the Guianas, Trinidad and the Orinoco delta of Venezuela. The tree averages 30–45 m. (100–150 ft.) in height with a clear bole of 18–24 m. (60–80 ft.) and a diameter of 0·5 m. (1½ ft.) or more above the large, spreading buttresses. Because of the large quantities available, attempts have been made to develop the export market but without much success.

General description. A very hard, heavy timber, average density about 1·03 (64 lb./ft.³), seasoned; not particularly attractive in appearance, being coarse textured with irregularly interlocked grain and uneven in colour, which varies from yellowish-brown to dull reddish-brown. Locally two or more varieties are recognised, based on the colour of the heartwood in the freshly felled condition, but it is doubtful whether these colour differences have any practical significance.

Seasoning and movement. The timber dries very slowly with considerable splitting and distortion. FPRL kiln schedule B is recommended. After seasoning, dimensional movement with changes in atmospheric humidity is large.

Strength and bending properties. Extensive tests have shown that mora is similar to greenheart in strength, though slightly harder. It is moderately good for steam bending.

Durability and preservative treatment. On the basis of laboratory tests and local experience the heartwood is considered resistant to decay and is classed as durable. Reports that the timber has proved unreliable in this respect may be due to failure to trim off the wide, non-durable sapwood. The heartwood is reputed to be resistant to termites but is not immune to *Teredo* and other marine borers. Preservative treatment is impracticable.

Working and finishing properties. Mora logs should be converted as soon as possible after felling to obviate a tendency for boards to spring off the saw when the outside of the log has become dry. The wood is hard to work and the surface tends to tear in planing. It should be pre-bored for nailing.

Uses. Mora is employed locally for heavy construction of all kinds except where it would be exposed to marine-borer attack. Typical uses are railway sleepers, framing and decking for bridges, wharves, etc., house building, fencing and heavy-duty flooring.

Other species of interest. *Several other species of* Mora *occur in tropical America, furnishing timber similar to* M. excelsa *in character. Morabukea (*M. gonggrijpii*) is an important timber tree in the Guianas.*

Mora

Quarter cut

Reproduced actual size

113

Partridgewood

[Caesalpinia granadillo]

Partridgewood is also known in Britain as maracaibo or maracaibo ebony and as granadillo, a name sometimes applied to cocuswood from the West Indies. In the USA it is known as brown ebony or coffee wood.

Distribution and supplies. This is a well-formed tree of medium size, up to about 23 m. (75 ft.) tall and 1 m. (say, 3 ft.) in diameter, found in Venezuela, from which the timber is exported in small quantities to Europe and the USA.

General description. An ornamental wood, dark chocolate-brown to nearly black, relieved by fine, regular markings of lighter colour, suggesting the markings on a partridge's wing. Extremely dense, about 1·25 (78 lb./ft.^{3}), of medium texture and variable grain.

Technical properties. The wood requires care in seasoning. It is exceedingly strong and hard and highly resistant to decay; relatively difficult to work, with a tendency for the grain to pick up, but capable of a good smooth finish on the lathe.

Uses. Partridgewood was at one time a favourite wood for umbrella handles. It is reported to have been used for policemen's truncheons and is suitable for such items as turned wooden knobs for doors and furniture. In the country of origin it is used for heavy constructional work.

Other species of interest. *A closely related species, sometimes confused with partridgewood, is brazilwood or pernambuco wood (*Guilandina echinata *or* C. echinata*) of the coastal forests of eastern Brazil. This is the only wood considered to be really suitable for bows for violins and cellos.*

114

Partridgewood

Quarter cut

Reproduced actual size

Flat cut

115

Peroba Branca or White Peroba

[Paratecoma peroba]

Also known as peroba amarella, peroba de campos and ipé peroba.

Distribution and supplies. A large tree, up to 40 m. (130 ft.) high and 1·5 m. (5 ft.) diameter, with a long, straight, clear bole. It is found in south-eastern Brazil, where it is in good supply.

General description. This is a moderately heavy, fine-textured wood of somewhat variable grain and colour but often with an attractive appearance. The sapwood is pale and well defined from the heartwood which, on exposure, assumes a warm, golden-brown colour. The grain is typically interlocked, giving a prominent, narrow stripe figure which, sometimes associated with a wavy grain, gives a decorative appearance to quarter-cut material. The density in the seasoned condition is about 0·75 (47 lb./ft.³), i.e., slightly heavier than teak and oak.

Seasoning. The timber seasons readily and well with little degrade, but twist and other forms of distortion may occur if irregular grain is present.

Strength properties. In most strength properties, peroba branca is similar to teak but is harder and stiffer and stronger in shear.

Durability and preservative treatment. The timber is occasionally damaged by pinhole-borer attack; once dry, the heartwood is rated very durable. It is resistant to impregnation with preservatives.

Working and finishing properties. The timber is said to be fairly easy to work, to machine smoothly and to take an attractive finish but, so far as is known, it has not been the subject of systematic woodworking tests. It causes skin irritation to some operatives.

Uses. In Brazil it is in general use for making high-quality furniture and for interior joinery in houses and public buildings.
In Britain it has given good results for vats for industrial purposes and for ships' decking. Figured logs are cut for decorative veneer.

Peroba Branca

Quarter cut

Reproduced actual size

Peroba Rosa

[principally *Aspidosperma peroba*]

Distribution and supplies. An important timber tree of south-eastern Brazil, up to 30 m. (100 ft.) or more in height and 1 m. or more (say, 3–4 ft.) in diameter, with a straight, slender bole. Large supplies are available.

General description. The heartwood is rose-red to yellowish, commonly streaked with purple or brown, becoming uniformly brown on exposure. Moderately heavy, average density about 0·75 (47 lb./ft.^{3}) in the seasoned condition; texture fine and even; grain variable, from straight to very irregular.

Seasoning. Peroba rosa appears to season without much splitting but some distortion may develop. FPRL kiln schedule E is suggested.

Strength properties. Timber of average quality is similar to oak in most strength properties but considerably harder. Where the grain is irregular the strength is correspondingly reduced.

Durability. It is classed as durable.

Working and finishing properties. The timber works fairly easily for a hardwood of medium density and does not cause undue blunting of tools. Irregular grain is liable to cause tearing in planing and moulding operations and in such cases a cutting angle of 20° is advised. It gives good results with standard finishing treatments and can be glued satisfactorily.

Uses. Peroba rosa is used in all kinds of building construction, including shipbuilding, and for joinery and plain furniture. Figured veneer is sometimes available.

Peroba Rosa

Flat cut

   Reproduced actual size

Purpleheart

[various species of Peltogyne]

Distribution and supplies. About 20 species of *Peltogyne* are known to occur in tropical America from Mexico to southern Brazil, but it is in the Amazon basin and the Guianas that the timber is well known. Many of the species are tall, slender trees with straight cylindrical boles, 15 m. (50 ft.) or more in length and 0·4–0·9 m. (say, 1½–3 ft.) in diameter. Supplies are ample.

General description. Purpleheart is among the most distinctive of timbers. Dull-brown when freshly cut, the heartwood rapidly changes to the vivid and well-known purple which, on prolonged exposure, tones down to a medium or dark purple-brown. It can vary appreciably in colour, weight and texture, the heavier wood generally having a darker colour and finer texture; variation in density is from about 0·80 to 1·12 (50–70 lb./ft.³), the average for commercial timber being about 0·88 (55 lb./ft.³), seasoned, i.e., about the same weight as Australian karri and slightly heavier than afzelia. The grain is straight, interlocked or occasionally wavy.

Seasoning. Purpleheart seasons well with little degrade; it dries fairly rapidly but with thick material moisture is difficult to remove from the centre of the planks. FPRL kiln schedule G is recommended. Once dry, movement in service is small.

Strength and bending properties. Purpleheart is a hard, heavy, tough wood, half as strong again as European oak in bending and compression, rather more than this in stiffness and resistance to shock and about twice as hard. It is moderately good for steam bending.

Durability and preservative treatment. An outstandingly durable timber, it is highly resistant to wood-destroying fungi and has a good reputation for resistance to dry-wood termites. Only the colourless sapwood is permeable.

Working and finishing properties. Purpleheart is relatively hard to work and offers a fair amount of resistance to cutting in most machining operations, due to its high density and because of gum exudation. Straight-grained material finishes well but tearing occurs in planing and moulding when the grain is interlocked or wavy and a 15° cutting angle is needed to give a smooth finish. It is difficult to nail.

Uses. Because of its outstanding strength and lasting qualities and the large dimensions available, purpleheart is suitable for heavy construction, such as bridges and dock and harbour work. It has proved highly suitable for chemical plant as filter-press plates and frames, under exacting conditions. As flooring it withstands most conditions of traffic. It is used for small turned articles and the butts of billiard cues. Despite its high density it can be sliced for veneer and is used in this form on a small scale for decorative inlays.

Purpleheart

Quarter cut

Reproduced actual size

Rauli

[Nothofagus procera]

The genus *Nothofagus* comprises the beeches of the southern hemisphere— important timber trees in the temperate zone of South America and in Australia, New Zealand and Tasmania. Of the eight or ten species found in Chile and Patagonia, rauli (*Nothofagus procera*), roble (*N. obliqua*) and coigue (*N. dombeyi*) deserve special mention.

Distribution and supplies. Rauli is found in the middle third of Chile, from Valparaiso to Valdivia. Mature trees average about 0·75 m. (30 in.) in diameter, with a clear bole of about 18 m. (60 ft.). Although supplies have been heavily depleted, rauli still ranks as one of the principal hardwoods of Chile.

General description. A reddish-brown medium-weight hardwood of excellent quality, resembling a mild grade of European beech in grain and texture. The average density is about 0·55 (34 lb./ft.^{3}) in the seasoned condition.

Technical properties. Rauli is appreciably lighter and softer than European beech and is generally slightly inferior to beech in strength. It is classed as moderately good for steam bending. Unlike beech, it is resistant to decay. The wood is easy to work, taking a clean, smooth finish, and is reputed to hold its place well when manufactured. It takes stain and polish well and can be glued satisfactorily.

Uses. In Chile rauli is used for the same purposes as beech in the northern hemisphere. It is the principal hardwood for furniture, flooring, cooperage and a wide range of joinery, and is also made into plywood.

Other species of interest. *The other South American species of* Nothofagus *resemble rauli in general character but vary widely in density and strength and are generally considered inferior in quality.*

Rauli

Quarter cut

  Reproduced actual size

Rosewood, Brazilian

[principally *Dalbergia nigra*]

The trade name rosewood, alternatively palisander (French: palissandre) or jacaranda (the Brazilian name), applies to a number of species of *Dalbergia* from different parts of the world. The wood of *D. nigra*, the principal Brazilian species, is sometimes called Bahia rosewood or Rio rosewood.

Distribution and supplies. The timber was formerly obtained from the coastal forests of Bahia and south-eastern Brazil. Owing to scarcity, supplies are now derived from further inland. The valuable decorative wood is cut from the heartwood of old trees. It is shipped in the form of roughly hewn logs, mainly for cutting into veneer, and as square-edged lumber, 19–75 mm. ($\frac{3}{4}$–3 in.) thick, 75–225 mm. (3–9 in.) wide, in lengths of 1·8–2·4 m. (6–8 ft.), occasionally larger.

General description. The heartwood of young trees is brown, unattractive and of little value. The decorative wood, as exported, shows varying shades of purplish-brown streaked with black. It is often oily to the touch. When fresh, it has a mild scent resembling that of roses. In the seasoned condition, the density is around 0·86 (54 lb./ft.^{3}), more or less, depending on conditions of growth. Texture is medium and the grain fairly straight.

Seasoning and movement. Like other species of rosewood, the timber should be dried slowly to prevent splitting and checking. Once seasoned, it absorbs moisture slowly and is dimensionally stable in service.

Strength properties. As would be expected from its weight, the wood is hard and has good strength properties, especially in compression along the grain, stiffness and resistance to shock.

Durability. Logs cut from old trees are often unsound in the heart, but the sound wood is very resistant to decay and insect attack.

Working and finishing properties. Brazilian rosewood is fairly difficult to work with hand tools. In machine planing it must be held firmly as there is a strong tendency for it to vibrate. The finish is improved if the cutting angle is reduced to about 20°. The wood turns excellently and polishes well.

Uses. Brazilian rosewood has been famous as a cabinet timber for more than 300 years. It still finds limited use, in the solid and as veneer, in contemporary furniture. The wood retains its popularity for the handles of knives and small tools, for carpenters' spirit-levels, butts of billiard cues, small parts of musical instruments, brush backs and fancy turnery.

Other species of interest. *Honduras rosewood (*D. stevensonii*) is denser and harder to work than Brazilian rosewood, and is preferred for the keys of xylophones and marimbas. Cocobolo (*D. retusa *and allied species), of Central America, is also considerably denser than Brazilian rosewood. The colour is remarkably variable; the bright hues of the freshly cut wood tone down to a deep-red, streaked or mottled with black. In the USA it is used for knife handles and, generally, as Brazilian rosewood. Kingwood and tulipwood (two other Brazilian species of* Dalbergia*) are described and illustrated separately. Other species of true rosewood of more or less importance on the world market are found in Africa (African blackwood and Madagascar rosewood), India and Java (Indian rosewood), Burma and Thailand.*

Rosewood, Brazilian

Flat cut

Reproduced actual size

Rotary cut

Quarter cut

Satinwood, West Indian

[*Fagara flava*]

Distribution and supplies. West Indian satinwood is found in the West Indies, particularly Jamaica, and in Bermuda, the Bahamas and southern Florida. It is a small tree, up to 12 m. (40 ft.) in height and 0·5 m. (20 in.) in diameter. In recent years the demand for the timber has declined but supplies can still be obtained through commercial channels.

General description. The heartwood is typically yellowish, becoming brown on exposure. As the name implies, it has a natural lustre and a fine, even texture. The average density is about 0·88 (55 lb./ft.^{3}) in the seasoned condition. The grain may be straight or irregular with a decorative figure, though it is less highly figured than East Indian satinwood. It has a characteristic scent of coconut oil which is apparent when the wood is worked.

Technical properties. This timber has not been subjected to the full range of standard laboratory tests. It is fairly hard to work, though not so hard as East Indian satinwood, and needs to be held firmly in machining. It takes a clean, smooth finish from the tool and is particularly good for turning.

Uses. This is the satinwood used by the famous cabinet-makers of the eighteenth century (the East Indian variety came into general use later). In modern times it has been used for small items of turnery such as bobbins for the textile industry, brush backs, marquetry, fancy goods and reproduction furniture.

Satinwood

Flat cut

Reproduced actual size

Snakewood

[Piratinera guianensis]

Distribution and supplies. Snakewood or letterwood is found in tropical South America. It has been exported to Europe from the Guianas since early Colonial times in the form of small logs or sticks, 50–200 mm. (2–8 in.) in diameter and about 2 m. (6–7 ft.) in length, with the sapwood removed. It is sold by weight and is one of the most expensive woods on the market. Nowadays it is of little importance because of its scarcity and the small sizes available; demand is strictly limited.

General description. Snakewood is remarkable for being the heaviest wood known; the recorded density is 1·2–1·36 (75–85 lb./ft.^{3}). Its appearance is equally distinctive—reddish-brown with irregular black markings suggesting hieroglyphic characters (hence the name letterwood) or the spotted skins of certain snakes. The grain is typically straight; the texture extremely fine and even.

Technical properties. This wood is extremely hard and strong but is brittle and splits easily. When worked it is inclined to splinter but takes a very smooth finish and a high natural polish. It is extremely resistant to decay.

Uses. Snakewood was formerly in demand for walking sticks, umbrella handles, presentation caskets and fancy articles. It has been used for violin bows but is considered inferior to brazilwood (see p. 114) for this purpose. It is sometimes sawn into veneers for cabinet work.

Snakewood

Flat cut

   Reproduced actual size

Sucupira

[principally *Bowdichia nitida*]

Distribution and supplies. Species of *Bowdichia* are medium-sized to large trees, up to 45 m. (say, 150 ft.) high and 1·2 m. (4 ft.) in diameter. The commercial timber is believed to be produced mainly by *Bowdichia nitida* which occurs in the Rio Negro and lower Amazon regions of northern Brazil; *B. virgilioides* has a wider distribution, from Venezuela and the Guianas to south-eastern Brazil, but over part of its range it is a savannah tree of relatively small size and poor form.

General description. Sucupira is a hard, heavy timber with a striking appearance, the dark, chocolate-coloured heartwood being relieved by paler markings giving a decorative appearance which may be enhanced on quartered surfaces by a stripe figure due to the interlocked and sometimes irregular grain. The wood has a moderately coarse texture and harsh feel; its high density, about 1·0 (62 lb./ft.^{3}), seasoned, approaches that of greenheart and places it in the very heavy hardwood class.

Technical properties. Information on technical properties is limited. As might be expected of such a heavy wood, sucupira is hard, strong and tough; little is known of its seasoning characteristics but it has a medium shrinkage on drying with a slightly above-average radial and below-average tangential shrinkage. The wood is difficult to work on account of its density and irregular grain but can be finished to a smooth surface. Sucupira has a high reputation for durability even under tropical conditions; it is extensively cut for railway sleepers and a small number used in the Netherlands showed no sign of decay after 17 years.

Uses. A strong, durable wood, sucupira is best suited for structural purposes and is, in general, too hard and heavy for purposes requiring much fabrication. As flooring, it splits badly under heavy pedestrian traffic but should be satisfactory under less exacting conditions. It has a decorative appearance and, though fairly coarse textured, is of interest for turned work and as a veneer for inlays in high-class furniture and cabinet work.

Other species of interest. *In Brazil the name sucupira or sapupira is also applied to species of* Diplotropis *and to* Ferreirea spectabilis. *The former has a superficial resemblance to* Bowdichia, *as described above. The latter is yellowish-brown and is better known as yellow sucupira.*

Sucupira

Flat cut

Reproduced actual size

Tulipwood

[Dalbergia frutescens var. *tomentosa]*

Distribution and supplies. Tulipwood is derived from a small tree of irregular growth in the Bahia region of Brazil. The timber is shipped from the port of Bahia in the form of round logs, rarely more than 2 m. (say, 6 ft.) in length and 50–200 mm. (2–8 in.) in diameter, free of sapwood.

General description. Tulipwood is distinguished from the various commercial forms of rosewood (allied species of *Dalbergia*) by its lighter colouring, yellowish to pinkish with red or purple striping, suggesting red and white tulips. The colours tend to fade on exposure. It resembles Brazilian rosewood in grain and texture but is denser, varying from 0·90 to 1·1 (56–69 lb./ft.³), seasoned.

Technical properties. The wood is generally similar to Brazilian rosewood but is somewhat harder and stronger. It is reported to be fairly difficult to work, is inclined to splinter but takes a high natural polish.

Uses. Tulipwood, together with rosewood and kingwood, was a favourite wood of French cabinet-makers, particularly in the Empire period, for inlay work and marquetry. Nowadays it is used to a very small extent for these and similar purposes.

Tulipwood

Flat cut

Reproduced actual size

Virola

[various species of *Virola*]

Virola has been marketed under many different names, depending on the country of origin. These include baboen, banak, dalli, tapsava, ucuhuba and virola.

Distribution and supplies. Virola is widely distributed in Central America and tropical South America. The principal commercial species are tall trees with straight cylindrical boles, averaging 18 m. (60 ft.) in length and 0·6–0·9 m. (2–3 ft.) in diameter above the buttresses. Supplies are plentiful and the timber has assumed some importance on the world market with the development of methods of minimising insect damage and fungal discoloration. It is obtainable from the Guianas, Colombia, Brazil and other tropical American countries, in the form of lumber and logs for plywood manufacture.

General description. A pale pinkish-brown timber of the light hardwood class with little or no visible difference between sapwood and heartwood. Without being decorative, it has a pleasing appearance, rather similar to gaboon (okoumé); fairly straight grained and of medium texture. The average density in the seasoned condition is about 0·53 (33 lb./ft.^{3}).

Technical properties. Laboratory tests on timber from Central America have shown that it dries rather slowly with a tendency to split and distort. Strength is of the same order as that of African mahogany. It appears to be unsuitable for steam bending. The wood is readily attacked by fungi under conditions favourable to decay, is susceptible to insect attack but is easily treated with preservatives.
It works easily with little blunting effect on cutting edges. Quarter-sawn material tends to tear in planing; a clean finish can generally be obtained in other operations if tools are kept sharp. It gives good results with the usual finishing treatments and can be glued satisfactorily.

Uses. Successful exploitation of virola depends on rapid extraction, conversion and antiseptic treatment to minimise degrade from fungal and insect attack. Well manufactured, graded material, reasonably free from defects, is useful for furniture linings and backings and interior joinery. It is also used for the manufacture of plywood and particle board.

Virola

Flat cut

Reproduced actual size

South American Timbers

SOFTWOODS

Alerce

[Fitzroya cupressoides]

Distribution and supplies. Alerce is found in central Chile where it forms dense forests covering large areas. The average size at maturity is about 30 m. (100 ft.) high and 1·2 m. (4 ft.) in diameter. The timber was exported to Britain during the period of acute timber shortage following the second world war but in normal times supplies are absorbed locally.

General description. Alerce is a softwood of unusual quality. The trees are of great age and exceptionally slow growth; the timber typically straight grained, free from knots and other defects, soft and light in weight, with a very fine, even texture. The reddish-brown heartwood suggests California redwood or very narrow-ringed larch (alerce is the Spanish name for larch). The density is widely variable, the average being about 0·42 (26 lb./ft.^{3}), seasoned.

Technical properties. The outstanding technical properties of alerce are its durability and excellent working qualities, which are similar to those of California redwood. The grain is so straight that boards and shingles of uniform thickness are commonly produced by riving the logs in the forest.

Uses. Alerce is ideal for carpentry and joinery, for light and durable construction of all kinds.

138

Alerce

Flat cut

   Reproduced actual size

Parana Pine

[*Araucaria angustifolia*]

Distribution and supplies. Parana pine is one of the few tropical softwoods established on the world market. It occurs mainly in Brazil and also in Paraguay and Argentina as a well-shaped tree, 24–37 m. (80–120 ft.) high and up to about 1 m. (3 ft. or more) in diameter, with a clean straight bole. It is regularly exported from Brazil in the form of graded lumber treated against worm and stain, mainly 25–50 mm. (1–2 in.) thick, 100–300 mm. (4–12 in.) wide, in lengths of 3–5·4 m. (10–18ft.). It is sometimes available also as plywood.

General description. The wood differs from the common softwoods of Europe and North America in its inconspicuous growth rings and consequently fine, even texture. The light-brown heartwood is usually marked with characteristic bright-red streaks. It is straight grained and the export grades are remarkably free from knots and other growth defects. (Boards cut from near the heart of the tree show leaf traces as darker spots; they are not usually classed as defects.) The average density is about 0·55 (34 lb./ft.^{3}), seasoned.

Seasoning and movement. Parana pine is more difficult to season to a uniform moisture content than most softwoods, particularly the darker material which dries slowly and is liable to split and distort. Owing to inherent stresses in the timber it is inclined to distort when re-sawn or machined. The dimensional movement in service is rated as medium. It needs to be firmly fixed to minimise distortion.

Strength properties. In most strength properties it closely resembles Baltic redwood but is inclined to be brittle and should not be used as a beam to support heavy loads.

Durability and preservative treatment. It is classed as non-durable, i.e., it is unsuitable for outdoor use without preservative treatment. The heartwood is moderately resistant to such treatment.

Working and finishing properties. The wood can be worked easily by hand and machine tools and takes a clean, smooth finish. A disadvantage is its tendency to spring from the saw when being ripsawn. It gives good results with glue and the usual finishing treatments.

Uses. Parana pine is largely used for interior joinery, particularly where clear material in widths up to 300 mm. (12 in.) are required. Typical uses are shelving, staircases, shopfitting, framing for kitchen cabinets, drawer sides, mouldings and gymnasium equipment. Considerable quantities are used in the vehicle building industry, for framing and flooring in light commercial vehicles and for the sides, ends and tail-boards of open lorries. In Brazil the timber is made into plywood.

Other species of interest. *Chile pine (Araucaria araucana) has a restricted distribution in Chile and south-west Argentina. The tree is sometimes planted in gardens in the milder parts of Britain where it is known as the monkey puzzle. The timber was exported from Chile to Britain during the period of acute timber shortage following the second world war, but in normal times the limited supplies are absorbed locally. It closely resembles Parana pine but lacks the bright-red streaks characteristic of the latter.*

Parana Pine

Flat cut

Reproduced actual size

Literature References

General

A Handbook of Hardwoods (Forest Products Research Laboratory, HM Stationery Office, London, 1956)

A Handbook of Softwoods (FPRL, HMSO, 1960)

Nomenclature of Commercial Timbers, including Sources of Supply. British Standards 881 and 589 (British Standards Institution, London, 1955)

Nomenclature Générale des Bois Tropicaux (Association Technique Internationale des Bois Tropicaux, Nogent-sur-Marne, 1965)

Tropical Timber. Statistics on Production and Trade (Organisation for Economic Cooperation and Development, Paris, 1967)

Canadian woods, their properties and uses (The Forest Products Laboratories Division, Ottawa, 1951)

Wood handbook (The Forest Products Laboratory, Madison, Wisconsin. *US Department of Agriculture handbook* no. 72, 1955)

Timbers of the New World. By S. J. Record and R. W. Hess (Yale University Press and Oxford University Press, 1943)

Properties and uses of tropical woods. By various authors. *Tropical woods* nos. 95–103 (Yale School of Forestry, 1949–1955)

The principal timbers of Jamaica. By C. Swabey (*Department of Science and Agriculture bulletin* no. 29, Kingston, 1941)

Notes on forty-two secondary hardwood timbers of British Honduras. By A. F. A. Lamb (*Forest Department bulletin* no. 1, Belize, 1946)

An appraisal of some Nicaraguan timbers. By J. D. Brazier and G. L. Franklin. FAO, 1967. (Spanish translation: *Maderas nicaraguenses.* Banco Central de Nicaragua, 1968.)

Surinam timber (Surinam Forest Service, 1955)

Forest products of British Guiana. Part I: *Principal timbers.* By D. B. Fanshawe (*Forest bulletin* no. 1, Georgetown, 1954)

Madeiras do Brasil. By J. A. Pereira and C. Mainieri (Sao Paulo, 1957)

Maderas y bosques argentinas. By L. A. Tortorelli (Buenos Aires, 1956)

Seasoning and Movement

Timber Seasoning (Timber Research and Development Association, 1962)

Kiln Operator's Handbook. A Guide to the Kiln Drying of Timber. By W. C. Stevens and G. H. Pratt. (FPRL, HMSO, 1961)

Kiln Drying Schedules. FPRL leaflet No. 42 (HMSO, 1959)

The Treatment of Timber in a Drying Kiln. FPRL leaflet No. 20 (HMSO, 1957)

(Literature references continued)

The Air-Seasoning of Sawn Timber. FPRL leaflet No. 21 (HMSO, 1964)

The Movement of Timbers. FPRL leaflet No. 47 (HMSO, 1965)

Strength and Bending Properties
The Strength Properties of Timbers. By G. M. Lavers. FPRL bulletin No. 50 (HMSO, 1967)

The Strength of Timber. FPRL leaflet No. 55 (HMSO, 1966)

The Steam-Bending Properties of Various Timbers. FPRL leaflet No. 45 (HMSO, 1958)

Durability and Preservative Treatment
Decay of Timber and its Prevention. By K. St G. Cartwright and W. P. K. Findlay (FPRL, HMSO, 1958)

Insect and Marine Borer Damage to Timber and Woodwork. By J. D. Bletchly (FPRL, HMSO, 1967)

The Natural Durability of Timber. FPR record No. 30 (HMSO, 1959)

Non-pressure Methods of Applying Wood Preservatives. FPR record No. 31 (HMSO, 1961)

The Preservative Treatment of Timber by Brushing, Spraying and Immersion. FPRL leaflet No. 53 (HMSO, 1962)

Working and Finishing Properties
A Handbook of Woodcutting. By P. Harris (FPRL, HMSO, 1946)

Machining and Surface Finish. FPRL technical note No. 5 (HMSO, 1966)

Uses
Wood in Building for Purposes Other Than Structural Work and Carcassing. (Timber Research and Development Association, 1963)

The Design and Practice of Joinery. By J. Eastwick-Field and J. Stillman (Agricultural Press, London, 1961)

Wood Flooring (TRADA, 1959)

Wood Floors (TRADA, 1959)

Timbers for Flooring. FPR bulletin No. 40. (HMSO, 1957)

Hardwoods for Industrial Flooring. FPR Laboratory leaflet No. 48 (HMSO, 1954)

Timbers used in the Musical Instruments Industry (FPRL, 1956)

Timbers used in the Building and Repair of Railway Rolling Stock (FPRL, HMSO, 1956)

(Literature references continued)

Timbers used in the Sports Goods Industry (FPRL, HMSO, 1957)

Timbers used in Cooperage and the Manufacture of Vats and Filter Presses
(FPRL, HMSO, 1958)

Timbers used in Motor Vehicles (FPRL, HMSO, 1958)

Timbers used in the Boat Building Industry (FPRL, HMSO, 1964)

Timbers and Board Materials used in the Furniture Industry (FPRL, HMSO, 1966)

Index

Contents of World Timbers Volume I

149

Contents of World Timbers Volume 3

Asia

HARDWOODS

SOFTWOODS

Australia and New Zealand

SOFTWOODS

This book is set in the Univers series and
printed in Great Britain by
The Journal Press (W. & H. Smith Ltd.)
Evesham, Worcestershire